Three Months with
MATTHEW

JUSTO L. GONZÁLEZ

ABINGDON PRESS
Nashville

THREE MONTHS WITH MATTHEW

Spanish edition copyright © 1997 by Abingdon Press

English translation copyright © 2002 by Abingdon Press

This book is printed on acid-free paper.

Library of Congress Cataloging-in-Publication Data

González, Justo L.
 [Tres meses en la escuela de Mateo. English]
 Three months with Matthew / Justo L. González.
  p. cm. — (Three months)
 ISBN 0-687-09455-0 (pbk. : alk. paper)
 1. Bible. N.T. Matthew—Textbooks. I. Title. II. Series.
 BS2575.55 G6613 2002
 226.2'0071—dc21

                                                         2001007892

Originally published in Spanish as *Tres Meses en la Escuela de Mateo.*

02 03 04 05 06 07 08 09 10 11—10 9 8 7 6 5 4 3 2 1

MANUFACTURED IN THE UNITED STATES OF AMERICA

C O N T E N T S

INTRODUCTION

This book is an invitation to study and to adventure. As a study it will require discipline. As an adventure it will offer new panoramas and exciting challenges.

Let us address discipline. Every important goal in life requires discipline. If a young person wishes to become, for instance, a doctor or a lawyer, it is necessary to follow, from an early age, a discipline of study and learning. If we are concerned about our physical health, we try to follow a discipline of exercise and nutrition. Athletes who prepare to compete in the Olympics must subject themselves to a rigid discipline for years on end. And yet, when it comes to spiritual life, very few Christians are willing to subject themselves to a discipline that will develop and strengthen it. With the excuse that we should "pray without ceasing," we do not set aside a particular time for prayer. And, since the Bible is always there, ready to be opened and read whenever we need it, we do not set a program of study. The result is that both our prayer and our knowledge of the Bible suffer, just as the body suffers when instead of following an ordered diet and a discipline of exercise we eat whatever strikes our fancy and exercise only when we feel like it.

The first thing that we need to do in order to develop a discipline of study is to set aside a time and a place. The studies in this book follow a weekly rhythm: Each week there will be six short studies and a longer one. If you then follow this study privately, you will require at least half an hour a day for the six short studies and an hour for the longer one. Consider your weekly calendar and decide what is the best time for you to set aside for study. Once you have done this, make every possible effort to fulfill that commitment. Little by little, just as it happens with physical exercise, that study rhythm will become more and more important for you, and the time will come when, if for some reason you are not able to follow it, you will feel its need.

If you are using this book as part of a Bible study group that gathers once a week, establish your rhythm of study so that the six shorter sessions take place on the days that you study in private and the longer one on the day in which the group meets.

On the other hand, don't be too idealistic regarding the time you have set aside for study. Life always has its unexpected interruptions, and therefore, very few people are able to follow a discipline of study without interruption. Sooner or later the day will come when it will be impossible for you to study during the time that you have set aside. In that case, do not be disheartened. That very day, even if at another time, try to study the material assigned for it.

A place is almost as important as a time. To the extent possible, have a particular place where you normally do your private study. This will help you avoid distractions. It will also be a convenient place for you to keep your Bible, this book, your notebook of personal reflections, and any other material that you may find useful.

The next important thing in developing a discipline of Bible study is the method one follows. There are many good methods for the study of Scripture. The one that we shall follow in this book consists of three fundamental steps: **See, Judge,** and **Act.**

However, before we discuss these three steps, there are two important elements that must be stressed, without which no Bible study can be productive: prayer and reflection.

At the very moment you begin each study, approach God in prayer. Ask that the Holy Spirit be with you during this study, helping you understand God's Word, and that the Spirit remain with you after you have completed the session, helping you to follow what you have decided. Always remember that even though you seem to be by yourself, you are not alone; God is right there with you. It is not just a matter of you and your Bible, but rather of you, your Bible, and the Holy Spirit.

After a few minutes of prayer, devote some time to reflection, reviewing what you have studied before. In particular, remember those decisions you have made in previous days. Read your notebook. Evaluate what you have accomplished. Ask God for the strength to go forward.

Move then to the three steps of **seeing, judging,** and **acting.** As you will note, the material offered under each study is organized according to these three steps. The first, **seeing,** consists of examining the situation before you. In the case of these Bible studies, **seeing** will be examining the passage itself. What does it say? Why does it say it? Who are the main characters? What role do they play in the text? What is the context of what is said? In this first stage, we are not asking what the text might mean for ourselves nor what it requires of us. We are only trying to understand the passage itself.

The second step, **judging,** consists of asking ourselves what the text might mean for us. Here, our personal experiences and our concrete situation become very important. We read the Bible in the light of those experiences and that situation and ask what the Bible says about them. Therefore, when this book invites you to **judge,** it does not mean for us to judge the biblical text but rather to invite the text to help us judge our own lives, situations, opportunities, and responsibilities. What does the text tell us about the church, about our faith, about our society? How does it affirm and support what we are doing and what we are? How does it question or correct it? What does the text call us to do or to be?

These first two steps lead to the third: **acting.** What we have seen in the biblical text and the manner in which we judge how that text refers to our reality requires that we act in a specific way. We do not study the Bible out of curiosity but rather to be more obedient to God's will. Therefore, the process is incomplete if we are content with seeing and judging. If we are to be obedient, we must act.

Acting can take many diverse forms, which depend both on the text and on our own situation. For instance, the study of a certain passage may lead us to greater commitment to the poor and the needy in our community. The study of another passage may call us to witness to our fellow workers. And a third passage may call us to greater faithfulness in our participation in Christian worship. Furthermore, **acting** does not always imply physical activity. In some cases, acting may consist in a further prayer of repentance. In other cases, it may be abandoning a prejudice we have. Sometimes the action may be very concrete and brief, for instance, calling someone whom we may have offended. In other cases, it may be a long-term decision, for instance, taking up a different career. But what is always true is that, if we really study the Bible in a spirit of obedience, the Word that comes from God's mouth will not return empty but will accomplish that for which it was sent (Isaiah 55:11).

It is important to remember that we do not read and study the Bible only to be *informed*, but also and above all to be *formed*. We do not read the Bible so much to learn something as we do to allow that something to shape our lives. Once again, the example of physical exercise fits the case. Whoever exercises does not lift weights only to see how much he or she can lift (in order to be *informed*) but also and above all to become stronger, to be able to lift greater weight (that is, to be *formed*). Likewise, our purpose in these Bible studies should be not only to learn something, to know the Bible better, but also to allow the Bible to shape us, to make us more in accord with the will of our Creator.

This implies that the method of **seeing, judging,** and **acting** should be more like a circle than like a straight line. What this means is that **acting** improves our **seeing** so that the method could be described as **seeing, judging, acting, seeing, judging, acting,** and so forth.

Every Bible study that we complete, each action that we take, will make us better able to move on to the next study. In order to understand this, think about a traveler in a valley. In that valley, the traveler sees a dense forest, a road that climbs a hill, and the position of the sun. On the basis of what he **sees,** the traveler **judges** that he is not to try crossing the forest but rather to follow the road. He also **judges,** on the basis of the position of the sun, in which direction he should go. Then he **acts;** he begins walking. Eventually he finds himself atop the hill, where he **sees** new views that allow him to **judge** the direction to be followed and invite him to **act** in a way that he could not have guessed when he was in the valley. Therefore, his **acting** took him to a new way of **seeing.** The same will be true in a Bible study. If we make progress, we shall see ever-wider views, and therefore, not only will our **seeing** and **judging** lead us to a more faithful **acting** but also our **acting** will clarify our **seeing** and **judging.**

What resources will you need to follow these studies? First of all, the Bible itself. Sometimes you will be tempted to shorten the time of study by not reading the Bible and reading only what this book says. The temptation will be even greater when the biblical passage is well known. It is important to resist that temptation. The purpose of this book is to help you in your study of the Bible, not to be a substitute for it. In the studies that follow, the Bible is quoted according to the New Revised Standard Version (NRSV). Therefore, if you use that version it will be easier to follow these studies. Naturally, if you have more time, you may wish to compare different versions in order to enrich your study. Some people following these studies have reported that they have used a Bible with large letters and wide margins so that they could write notes and comments. That is up to you.

Second, use this book. Try to follow the rhythm of studies suggested, reading and studying each passage on the day assigned. We are too used to living life in a hurry. Instead of cooking a roast for five hours, we place it in the microwave for thirty minutes. Sometimes we want to do the same with our spiritual life. If it is good for us to do one of these Bible studies a day, why not go ahead and do them all at once? Here once again the example of physical exercise may be useful. If you try to do a month's worth of exercise in a single day, the results will be very different than if you establish a rhythm of exercise and stick to it. Likewise, if we wish the Bible to shape us, to strengthen and to nourish our spiritual life, it is necessary for us to establish a rhythm that we can continue in the long run.

Third, you will need a notebook in which you can write down your reflections, resolutions, and experiences. Write in it not only what is suggested in some of the studies in this book but also anything that seems relevant to you. If something strikes your interest but you cannot follow up on it at the time, make a note of it. Write your answers to the questions posed in the book. Make a note of your decisions, your doubts, your achievements, your failures. Use it at the beginning of each study session, in the period set aside for reflection, in order to help you remember what you have learned and thought in the course of your studies "with Matthew."

Make sure that every time you begin a study session you have at hand all of these resources: your Bible, this book, your notebook, and a pencil or pen.

No other resources are absolutely necessary for these studies. But if you wish to study the Gospel of Matthew more deeply, there are other tools that you may find useful: (1) several versions of the Bible in case you want to compare them; (2) a good commentary on Matthew; (3) a dictionary of the Bible; (4) a biblical atlas. These resources will be particularly helpful if the seventh session of each week will be a group study and you are responsible for leading the group.

Finally, do not forget two resources readily available to you that are absolutely indispensable for any good Bible study. The first is your own experience. Some of us have been told that when we study the Bible we should leave aside all our other concerns. Nothing could be further from the truth. The Bible is here to respond to our concerns, and our experience and our situation in life help us understand the Bible and hear God's Word for us today.

The second such resource is the community of faith. I have already pointed out that when you study the Bible you are not alone with your Bible; the Holy Spirit of God is also there. Now I must add that, in a very real sense, your faith community is also there. The Gospel of Matthew was probably written to be read out loud, in the gathering of the church. Therefore, when you read it, even though you may be alone, keep in mind the community of faith that surrounds and upholds you. Read it not only as God's Word for you but also as God's Word for the church. That is why this book includes the longer Bible study each week: to encourage readers to use it in study groups. These groups may gather once a week, but during the other six days, you will each know that the rest of the group is studying the same Bible passage.

I said at the beginning of this introduction that this book is an invitation both to study and to adventure. On this last point, it is best to say no more. Adventures are best when they are unexpected and surprising. Plunge, then, into the study of the Gospel of Matthew knowing that at some point it will surprise you but knowing and trusting also that, even in such surprises, God is already there ahead of you, waiting for you with open arms!

WEEK ONE

First Day: Read Matthew 1:1-17

See: Read the genealogy of Jesus in these first seventeen verses. Mark the names of those people whom you remember from earlier Bible studies, sermons, or other sources. (Do not be discouraged. No matter how well you know the Bible, some of these names will be unknown to you, for they only appear in this passage.)

Now try to read the list as it would have been read by an early reader who knew the Hebrew Bible but not the rest of the Bible story. Note that in this genealogy there is a case of incest in the story of Judah and Tamar (Genesis 38:13-19), a prostitute, Rahab (Joshua 2:1-22 and 6:22-25), a Gentile (Ruth), and a case of sexual harassment and adultery in the story of David and "the wife of Uriah" (2 Samuel 11, Masoretic Text).

Judge: This is one of the least studied passages in the entire Gospel of Matthew. It seems to be no more than a list of names. Yet Matthew begins his Gospel with it. Why? Consider the following possibilities:

First, by including this genealogy Matthew tells us that the gospel of Jesus springs from the history of Israel. In order to understand Jesus, one has to understand the history of what God did amid God's people, preparing the way, centuries before. The birth of Jesus does not take place in a vacuum but is rather the culmination of a long historical process. Verse 17 summarizes that long genealogy, taking us from Abraham to David, from David to the Babylonian Exile, and from the Exile to Jesus. Jesus came to the world in the midst of a history, and we all come to Jesus in the midst of our own histories. In contrast, too often we tend to think that past generations have nothing to do with us. Sometimes we remember who brought the gospel to us. But we rarely think about all that took place before, and how, throughout the ages, God was preparing the way so that we might believe.

Second, by including all the skeletons in Jesus' genealogical closet, Matthew tells us that we do not have to hide the skeletons in our histories or in our own personal lives. Jesus, the heir to this genealogy, came precisely to free us from such skeletons. When we do take our history into account, we tend to dress it up with as much glory as possible. We claim that all our ancestors were great and honorable people. Above all, we pretend that we have done many great and beautiful things and few that are ugly, petty, or sinful. But it is not thus that the Bible tells the story of God's people nor the genealogy of God's own Son.

Act: Think about your own history in the faith. How did you come to faith? Who are your ancestors in the faith, whom God used to bring you to where you are today? What do you know about the history of your church and your place in it? What skeletons are there in the closet of your life and of your history that you try to hide? Have you brought them to the feet of Jesus?

Jot down your reflections.

Second Day: Read Matthew 1:18-25

12-19-04

See: Note the importance of Joseph in this passage. In other Christmas stories, Mary takes center stage, and therefore, we often think of Joseph as the background for the narrative. But in this story, Joseph is one of the main characters. The angel of the Lord appears to him in dreams and tells him about the One who is to be born and the name that he shall be given. Joseph had decided to dismiss Mary quietly because she was pregnant. But on the basis of the vision of the angel, he received her as if the child had been his.

Note also that the name of Jesus means the same as Joshua, "Yahweh saves." What Jesus has come to do is similar to what Joshua did in ancient times. Just as Joshua opened the way for the people in the conquest of the promised land so also does Jesus open the way for the people into the promise.

Judge: Remember that this passage comes immediately after the genealogy of Jesus. The story of Christmas is crafted into that genealogy as the high point of a process that God had been leading for centuries. When we forget the enormous significance of what is taking place here, Christmas becomes an empty celebration, or at best a celebration of beautiful sentimentality but very distant from the cosmic dimensions of these events. The Child who lies in a manger is the Lord of history. The Child whose birth we celebrate was present when the galaxies were born. We celebrate his birth because in him we also are born anew. We celebrate his birth because in him we are in harmony with all of his creation, with life itself. We celebrate his birth because it is by him that we have both our first, physical birth and our new birth in the Spirit.

In the midst of all this, the human and social insignificance of Joseph and Mary shows us that quite often the greatest actions of God take place in what appears to be small and even worthless. Joseph's answer tells us that God's action often requires of us extraordinary decisions and actions.

Act: If God has thus acted, consider the following: *When Christmas approaches, what will I be able to do to make certain that my celebrations show the magnitude of this event?* Think about the manners in which you, your family, and your church usually celebrate Christmas. Resolve to do at least one thing in order to make your Christmas celebrations closer to the great event of Christmas. Write it down. What does the birth of Jesus tell us about the value of that which is common or undervalued? Think about someone in your community who is not considered to be very important. Resolve to show respect and appreciation for that person. Write his or her name. Pray for her or for him.

Third Day: Read Matthew 2:1-12   1-2-05

See: Legend has added much to the passage we are studying. As soon as we begin reading this story, we think about the "Three Wise Men." According to tradition, these were also kings coming from different lands and races, and their names were Caspar, Melchior, and Balthasar.

But the Bible does not tell us they were kings nor even that there were three. Furthermore, the title of *magi*, which is the literal translation from Greek, does not imply that they were magicians, such as we see today in the theater or in the circus. Nor does it imply particular wisdom. It was rather the name given to priests of the Persian religion, who often were also practitioners of astrology.

Judge: There are at least three important points to take into account in this passage.

First, God brings to the feet of Jesus people who did not belong to the people of Israel and did not even know the Scriptures. Too often we imagine that in order to follow Jesus we all have to come to him by the same path. There are even those who make lists of experiences that one must have. But here we meet some priests of a religion that was alien to the biblical tradition who are led to Jesus through the observation of the stars. This does not mean that we have to go on looking at the stars, as do those who today follow astrology. But it does mean that we should not be surprised if God uses unexpected means to bring others to Christ. When such things happen, rather than being judgmental about others and their faith, what we are to do is acknowledge God's action.

Second, the Magi "were overwhelmed with joy." The proof that we have really met the Lord of the manger and of history is this great joy, which overcomes not only every other joy but also every pain and suffering.

Third, the Magi offer their gifts to Jesus. In a way, their gifts were not very practical. What could a child in a manger do with gold, frankincense, and myrrh? But that which they had they placed at the feet of Jesus, and therefore, throughout the ages the church has remembered and celebrated their coming from the East and their generous gifts. It is expected of us to give whatever we have, no matter how useless it might seem, as long as it is the best we do have!

Act: Make an inventory of your life and your gifts. Write down what you have. Write down not only things and money but also time, talents, influence, and so forth. Even though you write few words, take time to survey what this includes. Then look over the list asking yourself which of these things you have really turned over to the Lord and which you have not.

Fourth Day: Read Matthew 2:13-23

See: Read the story carefully. You will note that it has two parts. One part deals with the "massacre of the infants," and the other part tells of the exile of the Holy Family to Egypt and how, when they returned, they did not settle in Judea but rather went to Nazareth, in Galilee, because they were afraid of Herod's family.

Judge: What we are studying today is the result of the actions of the Magi. We often ignore this connection because we like the story of the Wise Men, and we do not wish to stain it with these consequences. But this is also in the Bible, and we must acknowledge it. The fact is that the Magi, because they did not know the political situation in Palestine, came to Jerusalem asking indiscreet questions, and the result was the exile of the Holy Family and the slaughter of the innocents. If the supposedly wise men had been more politically astute, they could have asked their questions discreetly, found Jesus, and returned to their land without creating any significant problem. But their lack of knowledge of political realities, and their apparent lack of interest in them, resulted in the deaths of the innocents and the exile of the Holy Family. Throughout history, one of the grave sins of Christians has been to be so preoccupied with other matters as to not take time to understand the reasons so many "innocents" suffer around us.

There is another aspect of the story of the Wise Men that deserves special attention: While the Magi are the ones who tell Herod of the time of the birth of the Child, "the chief priests and scribes of the people" are the ones who tell him the place (verse 4). Throughout history there have been Christians, and even pastors and theologians, who have acquiesced to injustice and have even used their knowledge of tradition and the Bible to serve the Herods of their time.

Act: Ask yourself: *Who are the "innocents" who suffer today?* Is it those who have no shelter in winter or shade in summer? those who flee tyrannies and terror? children who have nothing to eat? Write down your answers.

How can we make sure, as we follow the star of Bethlehem and especially as we celebrate Christmas, that our actions benefit these innocents rather than harm them? Write down your answers.

Take a few minutes to think about this. Make a list of possible actions you could take as you plan for next Christmas. Write down the names of other people with whom you should discuss these matters.

Fifth Day: Read Matthew 3:1-17

See: The last of the prophets announcing the coming of Jesus was John the Baptist. He is an austere figure. He lived in the desert, was clothed in camel's hair with a leather belt, and ate locusts and wild honey.

His message was a call to repentance. From very early times when prophets spoke of "the day of the Lord," they announced that it would be a difficult time, a day of judgment, and therefore the announcement of that day was usually accompanied by a call to repentance. John the Baptist is one in that long line of prophets. He too calls for repentance.

However, such repentance becomes particularly urgent because the day of the Lord is at hand. As he says, "Repent, for the kingdom of heaven has come near." As the advent of Jesus approaches, John proclaims that "the ax is lying at the root of the trees." The image is blunt. As a woodsman prepares to fell a tree and as he studies the best way to go about it, he lays the ax at the trunk. Then he walks around the tree in order to decide how to cut it. The tree has not yet received the first blow of the ax and may believe itself safe. But it is about to be felled. Likewise, the Baptist says, the judgment of God is approaching, and every tree that does not bear good fruit will be cut and burned in the fire.

Judge: Sometimes we think that the advent of Jesus is to be received with lots of noise and parties. Certainly, that is what our society does at Christmas. However, the Bible is much more realistic. In the Bible the first thing we are told as Jesus approaches is that we must repent. The Bible does not hide our sin behind the noise of parties or the blinking of lights. On the contrary, the ministry of Jesus is announced with the terrible words of John the Baptist: "The ax is lying at the root of the trees; every tree therefore that does not bear good fruit is cut down and thrown into the fire."

In order to celebrate the true joy of the Christian faith, we have to begin by acknowledging the misery from which Jesus came to save us. We have to acknowledge the need for repentance. True celebration must begin with confession of our own sin.

Act: As Christmas approaches, usually one of the first things you do is make a list of people to receive gifts. But in fact the first list we must make as we approach Jesus, be it at Christmas or at any other time, is a list of our own need before God and of the unmerited gifts we have received by God's grace. Write these two lists in your notebook. Go back to them often as you continue this study. Feel free to add other items as they come to mind.

Sixth Day: Read Matthew 4:1-11

See: We now come to the point where Jesus begins his ministry. It is important to note that this ministry opens with temptation. Jesus has just been baptized, and in that baptism he has received approval from on high (Matthew 3:17). But now, before he began preaching, "Jesus was led up by the Spirit into the wilderness to be tempted by the devil." Note that the temptation, while the work of the devil, does not come without God's knowledge. It is the Holy Spirit who takes Jesus to the wilderness. Note also that, in a sense, the temptation comes as a result of religious activity. Jesus fasted forty days and forty nights (which in the Bible is another way of saying "a long time") and, as was to be expected, was hungry. So, the devil made use of that situation for the first of his temptations. Note that the first two temptations have one thing in common: The devil begins by doubting Jesus: "If you are the Son of God." Notice that the third temptation also has to do with this matter of Jesus' identity, for if he worships the devil he will be declaring himself to be, not the Son of God, but a son of the devil.

Judge: Why do you think Matthew tells about the temptations of Jesus at the very beginning of his ministry? Could it be to remind us that it is precisely as we undertake the greatest endeavors that temptations also become greater?

Note that God's action is affirmed both at the beginning and at the end of the text. At the beginning, it is the Holy Spirit who takes Jesus to the wilderness. At the end, God sends angels to serve Jesus. Temptation does not come without God's knowledge. And by overcoming it we are strengthened in our relationship with God.

Note also that, frequently, temptation is a matter of identity. That is why the devil challenges Jesus: "If you are the Son of God." What the devil really wishes is not to make Jesus turn stones into bread or to make him jump from the pinnacle of the Temple in Jerusalem but rather to have him forget or doubt that he is the Son of God. The same is true of our worst temptations. Their power lies precisely in that if we yield to them, we forget or deny our own identity as children of God. That is why false humility is dangerous. If such false humility leads us to forget that we are children of God and that, as such, we deserve respect and justice, we are at the edge of yielding to temptation.

Act: Write in your notebook: *Because I am a child of God, I must* . . . Answer the sentence the way you think best. Do the same with two other sentences: *Because I am a child of God, I must not* . . . *Because I am a child of God, others must* . . .

Seventh Day: Read Matthew 4:12-25

See: Verse 12 sets the context for the events we are about to study. The ministry of Jesus begins precisely at the end of John's. John was his fore-runner, or herald. While he was preaching about the One who was to come, it still was not the time for Jesus to be publicly manifested. Since John announces Jesus, the ministry of Jesus begins with the arrest of John.

Also, the same verse tells us that he "withdrew to Galilee." If we read the previous chapter and the first eleven verses of this one, we will under-stand this better. Matthew says that Jesus "came from Galilee to John at the Jordan, to be baptized" (verse 13). At the beginning of chapter 4 we see that, after his baptism, Jesus did not return to Galilee but rather was "led up by the Spirit into the wilderness."

Capernaum, which is mentioned in verse 13 as the place of Jesus' resi-dence, was a city on the shore of the Sea of Galilee. It appears repeatedly in the Gospels, since it was the stage for a significant part of the ministry of Jesus, and apparently was his center of operations for some time. See, for instance, Matthew 8:14; Mark 1:21, 29; 2:1; 9:33; Luke 4:38; 7:5; and John 2:12. There are still some ruins in the area, which may be the remains of ancient Capernaum, and among them are parts of a synagogue, which may have existed at the time of Jesus.

The prophecy from Isaiah is well known, for it is regularly read in churches during the Advent season. The reference to "Galilee of the nations" (Isaiah 9:1) sounds a theme that will appear steadily in the Gospel. Galilee was looked on by other Jews as not truly Jewish. Galileans were second-class Jews whose faithfulness and purity were always in question. As may be seen as one reads the rest of the Gospel, part of the conflict of Jesus with the authorities and the people of Jerusalem had to do with him and his disciples being Galileans.

As you study the beginning of the ministry of Jesus as described in this passage, three points are apparent:

First, what Jesus preaches is the message of the kingdom or the reign of God. Throughout the preaching of Jesus the theme of the reign is central. The content of his message is described twice in the passage we are now studying: in verses 17 and 23. The first of these gives us a direct quote from Jesus, which was also the content of John's preaching: "Repent, for the kingdom of heaven has come near." In verse 23 we are told that Jesus went about "proclaiming the good news of the kingdom," or the *gospel* of the kingdom.

The message of Jesus is a proclamation and a demonstration of God's reign. The "good news" is not, as we often think, that in Jesus God forgives us. According to this text, the good news is the approach of God's reign. This, however, is good news that demands repentance. Why? Because it is an announcement of a new order. The ancient order, according to which people live their lives apart from God and God's justice, is passing away. The new order requires that we begin living as citizens of the new reign.

Second, the preaching of Jesus is joined to signs of the reign of God. It is a matter not only of inviting people to repent and follow him but also of showing them at least a glimpse of the new order of the kingdom. When the blind see and the lame walk, it shows that God's reign is breaking into human history.

Third, the ministry of Jesus also includes calling others to follow him and to share in that ministry. "Follow me, and I will make you fish for people." In these brief verses, at the very beginning of the ministry of Jesus, four people are called to share in that ministry. The calling of Simon and his brother Andrew (verse 18) and of James and his brother John (verse 21) is better known according to the more extensive version in Luke 5:1-11. Although Matthew does not mention the miracle of the great catch of fish, he does tell us the most important detail: that they left their business "immediately" in order to follow Jesus.

Note also that in a way the last verses of this text are a summary of the ministry of Jesus. Further on, Matthew will give us more detailed examples of the miracles of Jesus and of people who came to see him from the various places mentioned here in verses 23-25.

Judge: The ministry of Jesus touches our lives directly in two ways. First of all, it is ministry for us, for our benefit. What Jesus did, he did for us and for the rest of humankind. Second, it is a ministry that Jesus shares with us, calling us to take part with him in his work for the benefit of humankind. Both aspects of the ministry of Jesus are important. Without receiving his ministry, we cannot share it with others. Likewise, we cannot claim that we have received it without somehow sharing it. The purpose of this entire study is to help us understand both Jesus' ministry and ours.

This passage has two practical applications for our lives and for the life of the church. The first has to do with the manner in which we understand and proclaim the gospel. What Jesus preaches is not just repentance and conversion but repentance and conversion in view of the coming of God's reign.

Jesus says: "Repent, for the kingdom of heaven has come near." This is not some sort of generic repentance because we have done evil or because we have not made the best possible use of our lives. It is a repentance that is made urgent by the proclamation of God's reign. A new order is starting, "the kingdom has come near," and therefore, our entire lives under the previous order are under judgment and require repentance.

This situation may be understood by thinking about France during German occupation. Most people obeyed the existing government because it wielded power. But as the news of resistance against occupation spread throughout the world and invasion was prepared to free the French people, that news was also an invitation for those in France to join the forces of resistance. The news itself was a call to repent for having collaborated with the usurpers and an invitation to a new life in view of the expected victory.

Likewise, the preaching of Jesus—the Christian message—is the message of the reign. God shall reign. Weeping shall cease. Hatred shall cease. War shall cease, as will injustice. Those who hear this announcement are invited not only to repent but also to join the forces of resistance against pain, hatred, war, and injustice.

At the same time that he preaches the reign of God, Jesus gives signs of it, "curing every disease and every sickness among the people" (verse 23). Likewise, our announcement of God's reign must be joined to works that are in themselves a sign of that reign. Love, justice, and peace must be practiced as a sign of the reign and as part of the ministry that Jesus shares with us. Without such signs, our message is incomplete.

It is also important to remember the second application of this lesson. The ministry of Jesus includes the call to others to join in that ministry. Jesus calls people who are busy. Peter and Andrew were "casting a net into the sea." James and John were "mending their nets" (verses 18, 21). They had important things to do. Jesus does not invite them to follow when they have time. On the contrary, the text says twice (verses 20, 22) that they followed him "immediately." Jesus still calls his disciples to follow him and to share his ministry both in word and in work. Unfortunately, too many of us are quite satisfied with the manner in which we have ordered our lives and do not wish to have Jesus upset our order. What we are doing is important. Jesus had better call someone else who has nothing to do or that young man who doesn't yet know what career path to follow. But not me, for I have my business or career. But the fact is that Jesus calls fishers from their nets and accountants from their books. The call does not come to us at our convenience but at God's. Could it be that Jesus is calling us right now to an unexpected adventure of faith?

Finally, note that the word *immediately* appears twice. When Jesus calls, it is not a matter of waiting for a more convenient time. It is not a matter of waiting until there is nothing better to do. The disciples left their nets half mended. If that is the case, what steps are we to take right now in order to respond to the call of Jesus and to share in his ministry?

Act: In applying this passage to our lives, what we must ask is, how would we change our lives if we knew that God's reign was coming tomorrow? In order to understand the importance of this question, consider the following example:

Suppose I tell you that when I retire I shall build a cabin in the woods and spend all my time fishing, sitting by a brook and away from the bustle of the city. But meanwhile, when I have free time, I spend it at car races and never go fishing nor seek quiet places. You would probably have difficulty believing what I tell you about my dream of a cabin in the woods. In other words, because I do not live now as someone who expects a different future, you are justified in not believing me when I speak of that future.

The same is true with much of our preaching about the reign of God. We proclaim it, but we do not live as those who truly believe that our future is there. Therefore, we should not be surprised when people do not believe us. Our witness suffers because our faith is not reflected in life.

On the basis of that example, think again about the question, *How would I change my life if I knew that the reign of God was coming tomorrow?* Spend a few minutes thinking about it and write down your answer.

Having answered that first question, think about another: *Why not change, when we know that sooner or later the reign of God will come?* Think about the excuses that we employ in order not to act now as citizens of God's reign. Write those excuses down. As you think about them, if you decide that any of them make no sense or are not justified, cross them out but in such a way that you can still read them. When you truly abandon each of them, completely remove them from your list.

You may also wish to think about this in more specific terms. For instance, how would I change the manner in which I use my time? How would I invest my money differently? How would my career or occupation change? Would I still treat people the same way? Write down your reflections.

Now turn to the other central theme in this passage: that Jesus calls us to share in his ministry. This is closely related to the foregoing, for if we are not living as those who truly expect the reign of God, we will not be able to give faithful witness to it. However, we must go further than this. We must open ourselves to God's will and hear the call.

Write in your notebook the following question: *How am I to share the ministry of Jesus?*

Begin by thinking of a concrete action you may take today (or tomorrow, if it is already evening). Think, for instance, of a person in need and how you may respond to that need. Or think about a place where you may speak about Jesus. Resolve to perform that action. Write it down in your notebook.

Now think in terms of a longer period of time. To what sort of ministry may Jesus be calling you? There are many ministries, such as ordained ministry, visiting the sick, helping the needy, music, teaching. When Jesus calls us, he calls us to share in his ministry. Therefore, he must be calling you to some ministry. Do you know which? Write it down. Are there some possibilities you may explore? Write them down. Do you think you should speak with someone about this? Make a note so that you do not forget.

For Group Study

If your study involves a group of people who gather once a week to study, and if you are leading the group, make sure that in this first session together you set aside some time to review with the group their experiences in private study during the six previous days. Ask if anyone is having difficulty and explore with the group how that person may be helped. Give everyone a chance to express and share their experiences and thoughts that have resulted from their first week of individual study.

Toward the end of the session, lead the group in discussion trying to help the various members explore the forms of ministry to which the Lord may be calling them.

W E E K
TWO

First Day: Read Matthew 5:1-12

See: Today we come to the beginning of the Sermon on the Mount (which will continue until the end of chapter 7). The first few verses in this sermon are known as the Beatitudes. They received that name because nine verses, one after the other, begin with a word that is translated as blessed, but more strictly means *happy* or *fortunate*. In Latin the word is *beatus*, and that is why we call this passage the Beatitudes.

Surprisingly, when Jesus lists the things that make us happy, it is very different from what we would say were we asked to make a similar list. Instead of saying that the rich are happy, Jesus says it about the poor. Instead of saying that those who laugh are fortunate, Jesus says those who mourn will be fortunate. Rather than saying those who enjoy are blessed, Jesus says those who suffer are the ones who will be blessed. Rather than saying that fortune is in fame or a good name, Jesus tells us that the fortunate ones are those about whom people "utter all kinds of evil" (verse 11).

Judge: What is the meaning of this? Does it mean that Jesus thinks that suffering, persecution, poverty, and calumny are good? Certainly not.

In order to understand what Jesus tells us, we have to remember what we have already learned about the reign of God. Jesus is proclaiming a new order in which God will reign. In that radical change, moving from one order to another, what is considered profit under the present regime is really a loss, and vice versa. Those who do not enjoy the benefits of the present order will rejoice in God's reign.

Note that in almost all of the Beatitudes the verb is in the future tense: "They will be comforted . . . they will inherit the earth . . . they will be filled . . . they will receive mercy." However, the verb *to be*, as it refers to the fortune or blessedness, is in the present: "Blessed are." It is obvious that those who are persecuted, poor, or hungry are not happy and should not be happy in such circumstances. However, they are already fortunate, and in a sense they are able to rejoice knowing that their present circumstances will change. The Bible nowhere says or implies that it is good or joyful to be poor, to mourn, or to be oppressed. But this text tells us that even those who now suffer all kinds of evil may rejoice knowing that God's reign will come.

Act: We each organize our lives according to a series of values. For some people, there is nothing as important as money, and therefore they set out to find ways of making as much money as possible. Others seek fame and order their lives so as to attain it. Others spend their lives trying to become as important as possible, to have better sounding titles, to have more people at their command, and so forth. All of these are fundamental values by which the present order is organized.

Make a list of the things you most appreciate in life. Prioritize them. In that list, which you have written only for yourself, how far up does faith appear? If your faith were indeed your fundamental value, how would that change the rest of the list? Pray, asking God to help you place faith at the very top in your list of values.

Second Day: Read Matthew 5:13-16

See: Immediately after the Beatitudes, these four verses speak about the witness of Jesus' followers. These verses tell us that those who follow Jesus are, so to speak, the "avant-garde" of the reign of God, the salt that gives new flavor, and the light that announces a new day. The present sufferings are a sign of the joy to come.

Note that both light and salt have a purpose. Without achieving that purpose, they are useless. Light placed under a bushel basket does not shine, and tasteless salt "is no longer good for anything, but is thrown out and trampled under foot" (verse 13).

Remember also that in ancient times one of the main means to preserve food (especially fish and meat) was salting it. Therefore salt, besides giving flavor, also stopped corruption.

Judge: Immediately following the Beatitudes are the two passages, also well known, about the salt of the earth and the light of the world. In view of the promise of God's reign, those of us who have received that promise have a special responsibility to give to the world the flavor of God's reign and the light of that reign. In the world there are many flavors and many lights. It would be a simple matter to lose our flavor, that is, to adapt to the tastes of the present order. But then we would be worthless. It would also be simple, amidst so many lights in the world, to hide our own. But then we would not be fulfilling our purpose, which is precisely to be a light that shows the path to God's reign.

Think also about salt as a means to prevent corruption. Just as bacteria corrupts meat so does sin corrupt both the individual and society. And just as salt counteracts the corrosive action of bacteria so are Christians to counteract the corruption of individuals as well as of society.

Have you seen Christians doing this? If not, could it be that the salt has lost its flavor?

Act: Review the news stories that you have read or watched in recent days. Do any of them reflect the corrosive power of sin in society, which results in injustice? Ask God to show you how you and your church can be salt in the world, counteracting the corrosive power of sin. Choose at least one action or one point with which you will witness thereby opposing the surrounding injustice and corruption in the world. Make a list of people with whom you will speak, calling them also to give witness to the faith in the same context. During the days to come, discuss this matter with those people. On your notebook, next to the name of each of them, write a summary of your conversations with them and whatever questions have been prompted.

Third Day: Read Matthew 5:17-20

See: In this passage Jesus makes it absolutely clear that his teachings are not opposed to "the law" and "the prophets" (what we now call the Old Testament). Later in the Gospel of Matthew, we will see Jesus opposing some of the teachings and attitudes of some of the religious leaders. But here he warns us that such opposition does not mean that the Jewish law or the Jewish prophets were wrong. All of the law and the prophets come from God, and "not one letter, not one stroke of a letter, will pass from the law until all is accomplished" (verse 18). That is why Jesus warns his disciples that they are not to break "the least of these commandments" (verse 19). On the other hand, Jesus claims that he came to "fulfill" the law and the prophets. This is much more than obeying or following them. It means that Jesus himself is the fulfillment of the law and the prophets. Those who wrote and spoke in earlier centuries, inspired by God, were announcing what we now see fulfilled in Jesus.

The result of all of this is that, far from destroying the law and the prophets, Jesus calls his disciples to a greater righteousness: "Unless your righteousness exceeds that of the scribes and Pharisees, you will never enter the kingdom of heaven" (verse 20). (In the text to be studied tomorrow and the day after, Jesus will give six examples of that greater righteousness.)

Judge: Consider the two poles of what Jesus says about the law and the prophets. One: Jesus does not abolish them. Two: Jesus fulfills them.

Not to abolish them means that the law and the prophets are still valid. We cannot simply say that, since Jesus has come, the law is useless. The law is a word of God in which we see the divine purposes for humankind. On the other hand, to *fulfill* means that Jesus has already obeyed and fulfilled the law in our stead. The law is not a burden that we must constantly carry so that if we fail to obey it we are condemned. The law has already been fulfilled, not by ourselves but by Jesus in our favor.

Therefore, while we still obey and study the law, we are not slaves to it.

That is the greater righteousness which Jesus demands from us and offers us: The righteousness of Jesus himself, who fulfilled the law for us and in whom we are declared righteous before God. There is no greater righteousness than this.

Act: Think of all the ways in which you try to justify yourself before God. Think even about this discipline of study that you are following in *Three Months with Matthew*. Are you doing this in order to justify yourself? Or are you trying to be more faithful and obedient to the Lord who saved you? Write in your notebook, with very big letters: *I am saved by grace, and not by my own works.*

Fourth Day: Read Matthew 5:21-26

See: In this passage Jesus offers an example of how one lives according to that greater righteousness that we studied yesterday. This example has to do with the commandment not to kill. What Jesus tells us is that the commandment points to a deeper reality, for it is possible to kill without actually taking the life of another person. The law points us toward what God wishes from us, toward the manner and purpose for which we have been created. Therefore, it does not suffice to obey it externally; but rather we have to make it part of the very fiber of our lives.

On the other hand, note what Jesus here is claiming for himself. In this example, as well as in those that we shall study tomorrow, the laws Jesus is quoting are God's laws. And now he dares say "but I say to you." By speaking in this manner, Jesus is placing himself far above all his listeners. He is saying, *Moses told you this and that in the name of God, but I have an authority that is at least equal to that of Moses.* Therefore, the first thing we should see in these passages in the Sermon on the Mount is a dramatic affirmation of the authority of Jesus.

Judge: There is much that can be said about this passage. But one thing that is often said is actually the opposite of what the text tells us to do. Sometimes we are told that verses 22 and 23 mean that when we come to church, and especially before taking Communion, we must forgive our enemies.

That may be true, but it is not what the text says. Read the text again. It does not say we should forgive those against whom we have some complaint. What it says, rather, is that if someone has something against us, we must go to that person and resolve the matter. To forgive someone who has wronged us is relatively easy. It is much more difficult to ask forgiveness from those whom we have wronged and to try to undo whatever evil has resulted. Yet that is precisely what the text calls us to do.

Act: Read verses 23-26 once again. Ask yourself if there is someone who has something against you (that is, who has reason to complain about you for something you have said or done). It could be someone with whom you were curt. It could be an employee or relative with whom you did not deal with all justice and love.

Make a list of these people. Place a marker on this page in your notebook.

As you are reconciled with each of these people, place a check mark by that person's name. Do not remove the marker from your notebook until you have tried at least several times to be reconciled with all of them.

Fifth Day: Read Matthew 5:27-48

See: Jesus is still giving us examples of the greater righteousness which he expects from his disciples, quoting ancient laws and explaining what this means in each of these contexts. The laws that Jesus quotes are good laws. This is true not only of "thou shall not murder" but also of "an eye for an eye and a tooth for a tooth." Actually, this last law was a way to curb exaggerated and vindictive punishments. (Verse 41 refers to the right that Roman soldiers had to force the people from a conquered country to carry their burden for a mile. As a response to such an abuse of power, Jesus tells his disciples to go two miles.)

Please pay attention to verse 48, where Jesus speaks of God's perfection and then calls us to be equally perfect. Here, God's perfection is not a matter of immutability or some other philosophical attribute but rather a matter of God's perfect love toward all, which makes the "sun rise on the evil and on the good, and sends rain on the righteous and the unrighteous" (verse 45). Likewise, Christian perfection does not consist of obeying a particular rule or not committing a particular sin but rather in acting in love toward all, friends as well as enemies, those whom we like as well as those whom we dislike.

Judge: Here Jesus tells us that we are to love our enemies. Our first reaction is that this is impossible, for we cannot force ourselves to love someone. When it is a matter of loving those we don't like or those who harm us, there is little we can do to control our feelings. Even if we tell ourselves that we have to love, it is not easy to force ourselves to do this.

Part of the problem has to do with the manner in which we understand *love*. For many of us, love is above all a feeling. *To love* is the same as *to feel love*. Without such a feeling it is impossible to love.

However, love is much more than a feeling. Love is also and above all a way of acting. Suppose for instance that I find a wounded child on the street. Its condition stirs in me sentiments such as pity, mercy, or even ire against whoever wounded the child. But love will exist above all, not in what I feel but in tending to the child's wounds, taking it to a hospital, and so on. Even though I have no idea who the child is, I will be loving it through such actions. If I do not provide the necessary help, no matter how much I claim that I love the child, that will not be true. Love, rather than a feeling, is action.

Act: Who among your acquaintances is the person you most dislike? Decide to do something for that person as soon as you can. If possible, think about concrete ways in which you can act lovingly toward that person.

Sixth Day: Read Matthew 6:1-4   2-9-05

See: We now move into the second chapter of the Sermon on the Mount. For three days we shall be studying passages in which Jesus contrasts the manner in which "hypocrites" fulfill their religious duties and the manner in which his true disciples are to do so. Today it is a matter of almsgiving; tomorrow, we shall deal with prayer; and the next day, with fasting.

In ancient times it was customary for rich people, as they went out on the street, to have heralds, or people with trumpets, opening the way for them and announcing who was coming. And then, as they passed by, these rich people would throw small coins among the poor, who were expected to praise them for their generosity. Therefore, Jesus is not exaggerating in telling his disciples that in giving alms they should not "sound a trumpet before you, as the hypocrites do in the synagogues and in the streets" (verse 2).

In contrast to such people, Jesus tells his disciples that their charity is to be done in secret, in such a way that their left hand should not know what their right is doing.

Judge: The word translated as piety in verse 1 can also be translated as justice. It may seem incongruous to us to connect justice with almsgiving. When we speak of alms or of charity, we often mean a very small amount, perhaps a few cents, which we give to another for whom we feel pity. This was not the meaning of *alms* in antiquity, especially in Christian antiquity. Such alms often became considerable amounts, and they were seen as an act of justice. By it, those who had more than they needed gave it to those who were in need of it. By so doing, they were undoing the injustice of the present order, which made some be needy.

This should guide us in our understanding of our present offerings and works of charity. They are not to be *alms* in the sense of being petty or inspired by pity. Rather, they are to be the work of justice, for we realize that the needy have the right to eat, to be dressed, to work, to receive an education, and so on. If, due to the disorder caused by sin, society does not provide them with that right, we who are believers must at least begin to do *justice* by responding to these needs.

Act: Review your expenditures during the past month. (Or, if you can, look at your income tax returns for the past year.) Did you give as much as you could to those works of charity that seek to remedy some of the injustice prevailing in the world? Determine how much you will try to give in the future and to whom. Write an I.O.U. in your notebook declaring yourself in debt to that cause, person, or institution. Keep track of your payments on that I.O.U.

Seventh Day: Read Matthew 6:5-15

See: The passage may be divided into three sections: Verses 5-8 deal with private prayer; verses 9-13 are the prayer usually known as the Lord's Prayer; verses 14-15 are a commentary on part of that prayer. Let us look at them in order.

The first part is parallel to what we saw yesterday when we studied how Jesus told his disciples not to practice their almsgiving in public but rather in private. Here he tells them the same with regard to prayer. (In the passage to which we shall turn tomorrow, he will give the same advice about fasting.) Let us note some of the common themes in the three passages:

- All of them deal with good religious actions: almsgiving, prayer, and fasting.
- All of them establish a contrast between the true disciples and the hypocrites. (See verses 2, 5, and 16.) All of these hypocrites perform the same religious actions, perhaps even to a greater degree than the rest.
- In all three cases, what renders the religious actions of hypocrites valueless is that they do them so that others will admire them.
- The result is that "they have received their reward" (verses 2, 5, and 16). What they seek is admiration, and that they already have.
- In all three cases, Jesus promises those who perform their religious acts without seeking publicity or approval that "your Father who sees in secret will reward you" (verses 4, 6, and 18).

On the basis of some manuscripts, some translations say that God will reward us "openly." This has sometimes been used by those who proclaim the false "gospel of prosperity," claiming that if one practices almsgiving in private, God will make one rich in public or that if one asks God for something, God will give it openly. Jesus never promised his disciples that they would be prosperous, comfortable, or successful. What he did promise them is a place in the reign of God. Therefore, the "public" reward of which those manuscripts speak does not mean that God will make us publicly successful or prosperous. It means that on the day of judgment, when the Judge separates those who will enter the kingdom from those who will not (according to a text in Matthew to be studied later), these people will be openly acknowledged by God.

In the case of prayer, Jesus contrasts his disciples not only with hypocrites but also with the Gentiles (verses 7-8). In several cultures and religious traditions, it is thought that by repeating the same phrases or formulas, one touches God's ear. In antiquity there were high-sounding religious formulas that were necessary to use in addressing each particular god. There were even those who paid someone to repeat a prayer for them. Jesus rejects all of this. God is not a prideful king whom one only dare approach with bombastic ritual or special ceremonies. God is a "Father" who "knows what you need before you ask him" (verse 8). Verse 9 opens with the prayer that we know as the Lord's Prayer.

We usually read or repeat this prayer as if it were a list of petitions: (1) hallowed be your name; (2) your kingdom come; (3) your will be done; (4) give us this day our daily bread; (5) forgive us our debts; (6) do not bring us to the time of trial; (7) rescue us from the evil one.

There is, however, another way to understand the Lord's Prayer. We can understand it as a prayer for the coming of God's reign so that all the rest is not a series of separate petitions as if they were a list of things we wish but rather characteristics or signs of life in God's reign.

When we think of the Lord's Prayer in those terms, we see that it is not so much about us as it is about God and God's reign. The prayer begins by calling for the name of God to be hallowed. Throughout the Old Testament, the most important task of Israel is to hallow the name of God. Likewise, in the New Testament the center of the life of the church is to hallow God. Both in Israel and in the church, God is hallowed by means of praise but also, and above all, by obedience. When there is sin among the people of God, the very name of God has been profaned.

At any rate, the greatest hallowing of God's name takes place precisely at the point where God reigns, where all knees shall bow before God. Therefore, to ask for the coming of God's reign is also to ask that God's name be hallowed.

In a similar vein, it is possible to see how every other petition in the Lord's Prayer is also a characteristic of the reign of God. The one that introduces all of the others is "your will be done, on earth as it is in heaven" (verse 10). That is precisely what the reign of God is all about: having God's will be done everywhere, in heaven as well as on earth. When the reign comes, God's will shall be done. Meanwhile, we pray for its coming, and we seek to obey God's will.

God's reign is one of justice. That is why the Lord's Prayer continues: "Give us this day our daily bread" (verse 11). This petition does not mean only that we ask God not to let us go hungry. It is also a petition for justice. Actually, that phrase is almost a direct quote from Proverbs 30:8: "Give me neither poverty nor riches; feed me with the food that I need." This "food that I need," or our "daily bread," is our just portion, what is necessary for us, and what is truly ours. The author of Proverbs prays that God will give neither too little nor too much: "Or I shall be full, and deny you, and say, 'Who is the LORD?' or I shall be poor, and steal, and profane the name of my God" (Proverbs 30:9). This makes it clear that in both cases—either not having enough or having too much—the Lord's name is no longer hallowed. Therefore, to ask for our "daily bread" is to ask for the justice of God's reign: that we may have what is necessary but not too much while others have nothing.

God's reign is first of all forgiveness. If it were not for God's forgiveness, none of us would have the least hope to enter the kingdom. Also, it is justice. Therefore, the "debts" or "trespasses" to which the prayer refers are not only those sins we may have committed against God but also all cases in which we have trespassed the bounds of the justice that is a sign of God's reign. An example of this would be to hoard bread to the point where others are hungry. Whoever does such becomes a debtor before God, whose will is of justice. (In the final week of our study we shall see a parable of Jesus in which he explains this point by referring to two debtors.) The explanation which appears in the third part of our text (verses 14-15) clarifies this point.

Some ancient manuscripts conclude this prayer with the well-known phrase "for thine are the kingdom, the power, and the glory." This gives the reason for the entire prayer: The kingdom is already God's. Therefore, the prayer, which begins as an act of praise to God, calling for God's reign to come, ends with another act of praise: acknowledging that the reign is already God's.

Finally we come to the two verses that explain the foregoing (14-15). It is significant to note that, of all that is said in the Lord's Prayer, Jesus explains only this point. Thus, this particular phrase, having to do with those who sin against us, is central to the entire prayer. Jesus offers no further explanation about daily bread or not being led into temptation; but he does explain about forgiving as we are forgiven. Furthermore, he tells his disciples that this prayer is like a two-edged sword, for while it is true that God will forgive us if we forgive, it is also true that we are asking not to be forgiven if we do not forgive. Thus, forgiveness for others becomes crucial to the forgiveness that we seek for ourselves.

Judge: Why do you think Jesus explains nothing else about the rest of the prayer? Perhaps because one of the signs of God's reign, which we believers may begin to show right now, is a life of forgiveness. In God's reign there will be no weeping or pain. But that must be left for the future, after death itself is dead and we are in God's presence. We can and must try to eliminate weeping and pain; but even thus, the fulfillment of that promise must be left for the final coming of God's reign. Also, it will be a reign of justice, but meanwhile, we live in an unjust world. We certainly can and must oppose injustice and seek justice, but in spite of that, we know that injustice will continue until the reign becomes a reality. What we can begin doing here and now—and will continue into the life of the kingdom—is to forgive.

In a way, this passage is the other side of the coin to the one we studied three days ago (5:21-26) when we said that Jesus requires us to be reconciled with someone whom we have wronged. There it was a matter of asking for forgiveness and doing all that we could in order to undo our wrong. Here we are called to forgive those who have wronged us and to do so without waiting for them to ask for forgiveness or to undo whatever harm they may have done.

In both cases what is sought is reconciliation. In both cases we are asked to do all we can in order to achieve it.

The difference is in what we can do in each of those two cases. In the first, we can approach the aggrieved person, request pardon, and seek to correct whatever harm has been done. In the second, we can forgive without waiting for all of this to take place. Naturally, this does not mean that the request for forgiveness and the righting of wrong should not be sought. Ideally, every grievance should be rectified. But even when this is not possible, our duty as believers and followers of Jesus is to forgive. It is thus that we now begin living in the promised reign.

Note also that the entire prayer is in the plural. Jesus does not tell us to pray *my* Father in heaven . . . give *me* this day *my* daily bread. And forgive *me my* trespasses. This means that when we pray as Jesus wishes us to pray—even when we do it in private—we are not alone. We are part of an entire community that, no matter whether gathered or scattered, has the same Father, and therefore says, "our Father."

This community is the body of men and women, of girls and boys, who—thanks to Jesus Christ—can call God "Father." This community is the church. It is this community that Jesus addresses by saying, "Pray then in this way." This community lives through faith in Jesus Christ, and it is one because it has only one "our Father," who is in heaven.

But this community is one also because it is a community of forgiveness. Without being a community of forgiveness, no matter how much it recites and repeats the same prayer, it is no community at all, and it certainly is not the community of Jesus Christ. Hence the enormous importance of the last two verses of our text. If we refuse to forgive, our prayer works against us. If the church does not forgive, it is not a community of faith, not a sign of the reign of God, and not a true witness to the gospel. It simply is not the church of Jesus Christ.

Act: Think about someone who has offended you or has done or said something you did not like. Or think about someone you loathe. Pray for that person. Try to forgive him or her. Ask God for a spirit of forgiveness. Make a firm decision to continue asking for such a spirit until the day arrives when you have truly forgiven that person.

Think about your own congregation. Is it a community of forgiveness? What have you done so that your church may be a community of forgiveness? Are you one of those who talk and gossip about others? Are you one of those who, while not circulating such stories, listens to them? Or are you rather one of the "peacemakers" to which one of the Beatitudes refers? Write down your reflections and decisions.

Is there someone in your church who absolutely refuses to forgive others? Write that person's name in your notebook and make a point of praying that God will grant that person a spirit of forgiveness.

For Group Study

In order to study the parallelisms between the passages for yesterday, today, and tomorrow, divide your group into three subgroups. Assign one of the three passages to each subgroup. Read what is said about each of these on page 32, where five points of similarity are mentioned, and ask each subgroup to identify that particular point in its text. Bring the entire group together and ask why they believe that these similarities exist among the three texts.

In order to study the Lord's Prayer, begin by asking where the word "reign" or "kingdom" appears in that prayer. The group will soon remember that the prayer, as we usually utter it, both begins and ends with such references. Then ask how each of the various petitions or lines in the Lord's Prayer relates to God's reign.

In order to study what is said about our "daily bread," invite the group to open their Bibles to Proverbs 30 and read verses 7-9, asking them to see how those verses illuminate this particular petition in the Lord's Prayer.

Finally, when coming to the last two verses of our passage (14-15), ask the class to discuss the following two points: *Why is this the only one of all the petitions in the Lord's Prayer that Jesus explains?* and *What can we do in our own group, and in our church, so that we may truly be a community of forgiveness?*

After emphasizing that the Lord's Prayer is in the plural form, end the session with all holding hands in a circle and praying that prayer.

W E E K
THREE

2-9-05

First Day: Read Matthew 6:16-18

See: Today's passage is the last of a set of three contrasting the sincerity of those who serve God secretly with the hypocrisy of those who do it publicly in order to receive human praise. Like the two previous passages, this one deals with a common religious practice, in this case fasting.

Fasting was a common practice among the people of Israel. It was usually undertaken as a sign of mourning, repentance, or intense supplication. It was frequently a communal fast, in which all the people abstained from food. Slowly, especially toward the time of Jesus, fasting became a more private practice. As often happens with such religious practices, there were those who used their fasting as a way of claiming a greater sanctity. These are the people whom Jesus calls "hypocrites."

On reading this passage, note that although Jesus condemns the practice of the hypocrites who make it clear that they are fasting, he does not reject fasting itself. On the contrary, he tells his disciples that they should fast, but secretly and only in God's presence.

Judge: In many of our churches little is said about fasting, and hardly is it ever practiced. Why do you think this is? Is it to avoid the hypocrisy of which Jesus speaks? Or is it because we live in a society that leads us to think the most important things in life are pleasure and comfort and that, therefore, there is no place for a practice such as fasting?

Think about this last point. Is there any value in denying oneself some pleasures simply in order to conquer ourselves? Or should we give the body whatever it requests?

Act: If you have never done it, try fasting for a day. Do it without announcing it or proclaiming it. Be moderate about it so that your health does not suffer. For instance, skip supper one day. Instead of eating, spend the time in prayer. While you do this, remember that there are millions of people in the world who fast, not because they decide to do so, but because they have nothing to eat. Pray for them. Figure out how much you have saved by skipping a meal and give that amount to the church for a program that helps feed the hungry. Consider the possibility of doing this periodically.

Second Day: Read Matthew 6:19-24

See: This passage deals with wealth, but it also serves as a transition from the foregoing. Actually, storing up treasures on earth may be understood not only in the literal sense of holding money but also in the figurative sense of earning the praise of others. Thus, hypocrites who proclaim their almsgiving, their praying, and their fasting are storing up for themselves treasures on earth, whereas those who do these things quietly, only in the presence of God, are storing up treasures in heaven where the Father who sees them secretly will reward them publicly.

However, it is important to deal also with the literal meaning of the passage, which has to do with money, wealth, and property. What the text tells us in verses 19-21 is that earthly wealth passes, but the celestial remains. Verses 22-23 tell us that those who are looking only after earthly treasure become unhealthy because the unhealthy eye infects all of life.

Finally, verse 24 sets the question drastically: It is not possible to serve wealth somewhat and also God somewhat. One must choose between them.

Judge: Have you recently heard many sermons in which Jesus' statement in verse 24 is said clearly and sharply? Why do you think that in today's church there is so little preaching about the need to choose between God and wealth?

Perhaps you have heard a sermon on the radio or on television where you have been told that if one loves God, God will make one rich and prosperous. In other words, that it is possible to serve God and thus to increase our wealth. What do you think Jesus would say about such teachings?

Act: Read what you wrote in your notebook a few days ago about the things that you most value in life (the first day of the second week). Has that list changed at all through these days of Bible study?

Take a bill from your wallet. Put it on the table and think about what you can buy with it that would produce the greatest pleasure. Think about how much milk you could buy with the same money. Consider the pleasure you would receive by giving that milk to hungry children. Ask your pastor to give you advice on how to get that money to those children. Your church or denomination may have a program against hunger.

Even better, go to a home for homeless children and take the money for the milk personally. Write down your experiences.

Third Day: Read Matthew 6:25-34

See: The first words in our text are important: "Therefore I tell you." This means that what follows is in some ways a consequence of what has gone before. The reason we are not to worry is that we cannot serve two masters. Why? Because to worry is to become a servant of wealth; it is worry that leads people to spend their lives always seeking more wealth and greater security. Thus, when we worry in that way we neither believe nor trust in God.

The poetic examples that Jesus puts forth are well known: the birds of the air and the lilies of the field. The birds neither sow nor reap, but God feeds them. The lilies neither toil nor spin, but they are dressed in a glory that puts even Solomon to shame. This does not mean that food and clothing are not important. On the contrary, Jesus declares that "your heavenly Father knows that you need all these things" (verse 32). These things are so important that God looks after them.

Judge: Note that not to worry does not mean that one is to live haphazardly, allowing oneself to be led by the winds that happen to blow. What Jesus proposes for his disciples is not a bohemian life. Jesus does not tell us to stop sowing, reaping, or spinning. Jesus tells us not to worry. The opposite of worrying is to seek first "the kingdom of God and his righteousness" (verse 33).

The righteousness or justice (in Greek the word is the same) of God's reign has to do with food and drink, with clothing and shelter. It requires that all have such things and that no one take them away from another person. We have to not ignore these things but deal with them as people who serve God rather than wealth.

Act: Make certain that you understand that God is indeed concerned about food, clothing, and material things. When someone says or teaches or preaches the opposite, correct them. Note also that we are to seek the justice of God's reign. Even though we cannot describe the coming reign of God in detail, there is at least one thing we know: It is a reign of justice. Therefore, to seek the righteousness or justice of the reign is to oppose injustice. Consult with the other members of your church. Find ways in which you may oppose some particular injustice in your community. Make plans to do so, not out of anger or hatred but out of love for God and the righteousness of God's reign.

Fourth Day: Read Matthew 7:1-12

See: The text begins by referring to one of the most common problems of our life in society: judging others, and especially judging them with a severity that we do not apply to ourselves. When we say to another, "Let me take the speck out of your eye," quite often this is simply an underhanded way of calling attention to their defects while forgetting ours (verse 4). However, the text goes on to tell us that there are people who are unworthy of "the holy" (verse 6). Therefore, it is not a matter of acting as if no one had specks in their eyes and all were perfectly holy.

Verses 7-11 deal with prayer and trusting God. God gives good gifts. We should feel free to ask for such gifts. But verse 12 turns matters around by reminding us of our relationships with others: Just as God gives us good gifts, so are we to give good gifts to others.

Judge: Yesterday we saw that just as God's perfection is manifest in the sun that shines over good and evil people, Christian perfection lies in loving all, including enemies. Today, the message is similar. Just as God gives us the best things, we are also to give the best to others. Unfortunately, one of the favorite pastimes of society is judging others, and judging them with a much stricter measure than the one we apply to ourselves.

The first thing we must do is look at our own sin. Once we have done this, we will be able to help the neighbor who has a speck in his or her eye. Our own sin, the log in our eye, makes it difficult for us to see clearly in order to help others in the midst of their own sin. On the other hand, having acknowledged and confessed our own sin enables us to help others. Having removed the log from our eye we shall be able to judge correctly. Although verse 1 says "do not judge," it is clear that Jesus is not telling us to abstain from every sort of judgment. That is why verse 6 includes those strange words about "dogs" and "swine." There are situations in which good judgment tells us that some people are not ready to hear the message.

Act: Try to remember a time in which you felt you were being unjustly judged. It could be a very recent experience or something that happened in your childhood. Now think about an occasion where you judged someone and then discovered your judgment was mistaken.

Write in your notebook in big letters: *Before judging another person, I shall apply the same measure to myself.* Repeat that resolution to yourself several times during the day.

Fifth Day: Read Matthew 7:13-23

See: On examining the text, you will note a series of contrasts: narrow gate/wide gate, hard road/easy road, sheep/wolves, grapes/thorns, figs/thistles, good tree/bad tree, good fruit/bad fruit, only the one who does/everyone who says.

The conclusion of these and many other contrasts is found in verses 22-23, where we are told that those who follow the second option will not enter the kingdom of heaven.

Judge: Jesus presents two alternatives: the hard road and the easy road; the narrow gate and the wide gate. Whoever says to him "Lord, Lord," but does not do the will of God is in the same condition as those who reject him openly. There is no middle category of "almost believers." Furthermore, those who act as sheep but really are not, are in fact "ravenous wolves."

Sometimes we would like to have a third alternative. It would be so much more pleasant to be able to opt for a form of Christianity that would allow us to choose where and when to obey and where and when not to. Sometimes we are even told that in order to follow Christ it is enough to raise your hand and come forward. But at best, that is only the beginning. Then comes the narrow gate and the hard road, which can be very long. There is the road of discipleship with all its disciplines and demands. The very harsh word of Jesus in this passage is that without the narrow gate and the hard road, without discipleship and its demands, there is no true Christianity.

Act: Review what you have done, said, and thought during the last three or four days. Remember particularly those moments in which you allowed yourself to be swayed by the circumstances of the moment, when you did or said something you should not have simply because it was easier (or, as Jesus would have said, because that path was wider). In your notebook, write down those acts of disobedience you remember. Try to discern whether there is a pattern to your actions, something that has become habitual, for instance, lying in order to get out of a difficult situation or speaking ill of others. Pray to God that you may be freed from those sins and habits. Make a resolution to avoid them. Think of someone you can trust with these faults so that this person may help and support you along the hard road of discipleship.

○ ⟓ ⟶ Sixth Day: Read Matthew 7:24-29

See: We come to the end of the Sermon on the Mount. This sermon concludes with another contrast. It is now a matter of the contrast between two people who each build a house. One was careful and built on a solid foundation. The other was a foolish man who built his house on the sand. As was to be expected, the house of the foolish man collapsed. Jesus compares these two attitudes with two possible responses to his hearers: being wise and obedient or being foolish and ignoring what he has said.

Finally, Matthew adds another contrast: that between Jesus, who taught "as one having authority," and the scribes, who, although they knew the Scriptures quite well, did not have authority.

Judge: Human beings seem to be builders by nature. We all like to build as if our lives were only about building. Some construct buildings. Others build corporations and institutions. Still others build dreams. But all of these will someday topple, like houses built on sand.

Think for instance about the largest and most solid building in your town. How long do you think it may last? What will happen then?

The only construction that lasts eternally is that which is built on the "rock of ages," for, as Paul would say, "no one can lay any foundation other than the one that has been laid; that foundation is Jesus Christ" (1 Corinthians 3:11).

On what foundation is your life built? How much of it will resist the ravages of time and trouble?

Act: As we reach the end of our study of the Sermon on the Mount, it is time to review what we have learned and to take stock of where we are.

Turn your notebook back to the beginning of last week. Read over your decisions and resolutions. As you do this, take note of what you have been able to keep and also those points that seem to have been forgotten or in which you have returned to your previous ways.

Write two lists on your notebook. Head one with the words: *I thank God that* . . . and under that heading list all that you see of improvement in your Christian life. As a heading for the other, write: *I ask God that* . . . and under that heading write those points or issues where you see that you need God's help in order to continue your progress in the Christian life.

End your session with a prayer, using these two lists as an outline for your prayer.

Seventh Day: Read Matthew 8:1-13

See: We now return to the ministry of Jesus. Today's passage tells of two separate episodes, which take place in different places. The first (verses 1-4) apparently happens immediately after the Sermon on the Mount, in an undetermined place. The second (verses 5-13) takes place in Capernaum. Both deal with people who approach Jesus in faith, asking for health for someone. In both, Jesus agrees to the request, and the person is healed.

In the first case it is the sick man himself who comes to Jesus. He is a leper. In order to understand the significance of this point, it is important to remember that at that time leprosy was feared as an incurable disease. A leper was cast out of society so that others would not be contaminated. The leper was unclean and untouchable. Many thought that leprosy was a form of punishment for sin (if not the sin of the leper, then the sin of one of the leper's ancestors). This makes verse 3 particularly poignant: "He stretched out his hand and touched him." To touch a leper was an extraordinary thing to do. It was an extreme act of mercy; it was a great risk. From the religious point of view, those who touched a leper were themselves unclean. The leper himself must have been surprised that Jesus touched him.

Once the leper is cured, Jesus tells him not to tell it to anyone but to go and do what the law commands when a leper is cleansed (see Leviticus 14). His purpose is not to astonish people with miraculous cures. He tells the leper that he is to do this "as a testimony to them." Although the text does not spell out to whom Jesus refers when he says "them," they apparently are the priests and the religious hierarchy. Eventually that hierarchy would reject Jesus; but he still wants them to hear his witness.

The second episode is quite different. The one who approaches Jesus is not ill. Nor is he a person despised by society. On the other hand, he is neither a Jew nor a particularly religious person by Jewish standards. He is a Roman centurion, a pagan. He comes to ask healing for his servant. Jesus offers to go with him. Like the act of touching a leper, this too was unexpected. A Jewish teacher visiting the house of a Gentile officer would be seen as an enemy of the people and would certainly be suspected of having touched or shared in things that the law declared unclean. Yet Jesus offers to go. The centurion tells him that this is not necessary, for he knows that Jesus has the authority to order that the servant be healed even at a distance. Jesus praises him for his faith and declares that the faith of this pagan centurion is greater than that of the children of Israel. From that moment, the servant is healed.

The two miracles offer some interesting contrasts. In the first case the one who comes to Jesus is a leper, that is, a person whom society considers unclean and worthless. In the other case it is a centurion, that is, an officer of the imperial occupation army. In the first case, the contact between Jesus and the man who is diseased is direct; in the second case, there is no contact except through the centurion. In the first case, Jesus orders the healed leper to present himself to the priest, as stipulated by the law in Leviticus 14, and tell him about the miracle that has taken place. In the second case, Jesus tells the healthy man who is present that the miracle has taken place to the benefit of the sick man.

In the first case, a child of Israel is healed and sent to the religious authorities of Israel "as a testimony to them." In the second, the faith of a Gentile gives Jesus the occasion to lament the lack of faith in Israel itself. In both cases, Jesus has compassion for the sick, and heals them.

Finally, responding to the faith of the centurion, Jesus comments that there can be greater faith among the Gentiles than among the people of God, and he announces that this is a sign of the manner in which Gentiles will come from all parts of the world and will be joint heirs with Abraham, Isaac, and Jacob in the kingdom of heaven (verse 11).

Jesus employs that opportunity to speak about how faith can produce children of Abraham among those who are not such according to the flesh. One can imagine that such words would not be well received by the Jews of that time. They thought their special relationship with God was guaranteed by their inheritance; and now Jesus tells them that "many will come from east and west," and that the "heirs of the kingdom will be thrown into the outer darkness" (verses 11, 12). In view of such words, and many similar ones, it is not surprising that many of the religious leaders of Israel would eventually turn against Jesus.

Judge: The main point to be drawn from this text is that the salvation that Jesus offers is holistic. Jesus is concerned about people's well-being, both physical and spiritual. This is not new but is rather the continuation of what may be seen throughout the entire Old Testament, where God shows concern over the well-being and the health of the people.

Too often we think that God is interested only in things spiritual. If that were the case, we would have to dispose of a large portion of Scripture, where God is declared to be creator of all things, the ruler of the history of Israel who liberates the people from Egypt, guides them through the desert, and requires from them not only worship but also justice.

The holistic nature of salvation may be seen in the very word that the Greek New Testament employs for it *(sotería)*, which today is what we mean by *salvation* and *health*. This means that one cannot make a rigid distinction between the *salvation* of the soul and the *health* of the body. Therefore, rather than thinking that *salvation* is important and that *health* is not, we are to think that our God—the God who loves us in body and soul—does not wish us to suffer, be it physically or spiritually. Physical health is part of the work and message of Jesus Christ.

Obviously, this does not mean that Christians will escape illness. We are not living in God's reign yet, and while we await the fulfillment of the divine purposes, we are still living in a world of suffering, of disease, and of sin. Everyone becomes ill, and everyone eventually dies; but Christians believe in the resurrection. And because we believe in the resurrection of the body, we also know that God is interested in our present physical health just as God is also interested in our spiritual health.

If we are truly to give witness to our faith in a coming kingdom of God in which there will be no more pain, death, or illness, we must give that witness by opposing every pain, death, and illness. Christian efforts to help those who suffer are part of the proclamation of the gospel. We announce a full salvation of body as well as of soul. Not to do this would be tantamount to declaring that while the soul belongs to God, the body does not. That is contrary to the clear teaching of Scripture.

All of this should help set our agenda as Christians and as a church. If salvation were only a matter of the soul, all that we would have to do would be to announce that salvation and invite people to be converted and saved. But if salvation has to do with God's reign and that reign includes the body as well as the soul, a full preaching of a full salvation must deal not only with people's spiritual well-being but also with their physical well-being.

Unfortunately, not realizing the holistic nature of salvation has led to absurd divisions of opinion among Christians. Thus, there are some who think the money and effort we spend in schools, hospitals, clinics, shelters for the homeless, and food for the hungry should be employed in the preaching of the gospel. On the other hand, there are those who think the resources we devote to preaching and inviting people to accept Jesus as their Savior should be invested in improving their conditions of life. Both are wrong because both limit God's salvation.

Human beings, as God's creatures, are neither disembodied souls nor soulless bodies. Human beings are a single, integral reality. The reign of God is a holistic promise. Salvation is holistic. Any "gospel" that does not deal with both the spiritual and the physical needs of people is not the gospel of Jesus Christ.

The biblical passage reminds us that we must not think that our salvation is assured simply because we are believers. The case of the centurion and the manner in which Jesus comments on his faith are to be applied not only to ancient Israel but also to today's Christians.

This other point is closely related to the first. The Jews did not have a guaranteed place in God's reign simply because they were Jews. Nor do we have such a guarantee for the mere reason of calling ourselves Christians or belonging to the church. Were Jesus to stand in our midst he probably would not like much of what he would see about our own religiosity, and he would probably tell us that we lack true faith as well as works of love. In order to be participants of God's reign, we must live by the promise of that reign and do the works that show that we truly believe the future lies in it.

Act: Seldom do we see miracles as surprising as those about which we read in today's passage. But quite often we do see people with needs similar to those reflected in that passage. As Christians, we must pray for miracles, but we must also pray and offer ourselves so that we may be the miracle that someone else needs. Otherwise, we are simply shuffling onto God's shoulders responsibilities that we do not wish to carry.

Remembering what we read earlier about the log in our own eye, begin by confessing your own needs and your sins. Ask God to give you what you lack so that you may be faithful to Jesus and manifest his love to the world.

Think of two people in need whom you know or whom you have seen. One of them should be someone who has physical needs, such as food, shelter, employment, or clothing. The other person should be someone whose needs appear to be mostly spiritual, such as faith, comfort, or love.

Write down in your notebook the names of these two people (or, if you don't know their names, at least something to remind you who they are). Think about how you may respond to the needs they seem to have. Resolve to be a response, and write it down in your notebook.

If possible, talk to others in the church about these needs that you have seen and how among several of you it may be possible to respond to them. For instance, if someone in the area is unemployed, perhaps among several members of the church you may find employment for that person several days a week. Do not do this expecting a reward nor even expecting the person to become a Christian if he or she is not one. Do invite the person to believe in Jesus, but if that belief is not forthcoming, rejoice in the good work that has been performed. Remember that Jesus healed many who were not grateful, and in spite of that, he continued healing.

For Group Study

If you are following these studies in a group, your discussion could revolve around the following questions:

Who in our society is like the leper, who suffers great pain and whom most see with contempt and no one will touch?

On the basis of today's Scripture, what do we think Jesus would do if he were to meet such a person?

What do we think Jesus requires of us regarding such people?

If we know that such is what Jesus wishes us to do yet we do not do it, what is holding us back?

Is our witness believable if we do not do what Jesus commands?

What can we do to make our witness more believable? What can we do as individuals? What can we do as a church?

W E E K
FOUR

First Day: Read Matthew 8:14-22

See: Today's passage naturally divides into two sections:

1. Verses 14-17 continue with the subject of the healing miracles of Jesus. Besides the specific case of Peter's mother-in-law (which, by the way, means that he was or had been married), we are told of "many who were possessed of demons" and of "all who were sick." At the end of this session, Matthew offers a theological explanation of the events, declaring that in doing these things, Jesus was fulfilling the prophecy of Isaiah 53:4.

2. Verses 18-22 revolve around two people who offered themselves to follow Jesus. One of them was a scribe, that is, a professional student of Scripture. All that we are told about the other is that he was one of Jesus' disciples. To the first, Jesus responds that life following him will not be easy, for he does not even have a place to call his own. To the second one he says that when it is a matter of following him, even the most urgent commitments become secondary.

Judge: Considering the first part of the text and the prophecy from Isaiah, note how we usually use this prophecy to say that Jesus took our sin and freed us from our guilt, but in this case the prophecy is made to refer to physical health.

Do you see any connection between this and what was said yesterday about the holistic character of salvation?

Look now at the second part of the text. When Jesus says that he "has nowhere to lay his head," do you think that he is complaining? Or is he rather telling the scribe that it is not easy to follow him? When he says to the other disciple, "let the dead bury their own dead," what does this mean? It certainly does not mean that the dead are literally going to bury others. Nor does it mean that the dead should not be buried. What it means is that there is nothing, no matter how important or urgent it may seem, that takes priority over the call of Jesus.

Act: A few days ago you made a list of things that you value. Ask yourself this question: *Are any of these things an obstacle in my following Jesus?* If the answer is yes, what you are actually saying is that whatever this is, even though it may be good in itself, it has become evil for you. Ask God to help you place things where they belong in your order of priorities so that those good things, which God has given, may be truly good and be an aid in your discipleship. Write down your reflections.

Second Day: Read Matthew 8:23-34

See: Matthew continues to tell us about two more miracles of Jesus. The first is the calming of the storm on the Sea of Galilee. Note that the disciples have some faith, for they ask Jesus to save them. But Jesus tells them that they are "of little faith." The second miracle is the healing of two Gadarene demoniacs. This passage is parallel to others that appear in Mark 5 and Luke 8, although in those passages there is only one demoniac. At any rate, the result is the same: The sick are healed, but their madness—the demons—goes into a herd of swine that then jump into the sea and drown. Upon learning of what has happened, the people of the area ask Jesus to leave.

Judge: How can you explain that even though the disciples ask Jesus to save them he tells them they have little faith? Consider this possible answer: A faith that is always concerned about itself is weak. Such faith, even though it knows that the Lord can save, does not truly trust that such salvation will indeed come. A deeper and more mature faith leads us to a trust such that one's own salvation is no longer a reason for anxiety or fear.

Compare the manner in which people respond to Jesus (1) when he simply heals the sick and (2) when that healing work hurts their economic interests (in this case, of the owners of the herd).

Note that quite often when good is done to some, others are disturbed and even protest. For instance, in a certain city a church began to bring cheaper food to sell in a poor neighborhood, and the merchants in the area became quite upset. In another city a church began offering transportation to elderly people in need, and taxi drivers withdrew from the church.

Is there good work in your community in which your church could be involved but is not because there is fear of those whose interests would be hurt?

Act: It is quite likely that your answer to the last question is that there are indeed such good works needing to be done. In that case, decide to learn more about the matter. Make certain that there is a true need. If there is, try to awaken the consciousness of others in the church so that you may act together. As a group, study the reasons why some would oppose such an action.

Are such reasons justified, or are those who propose them only defending their own interests or prejudices?

If we do not act, is there a chance that this is because we are people of little faith, like the disciples?

Prayerfully consider the best course to take.

Third Day: Read Matthew 9:1-8

See: You probably know this story better according to the account in Mark 2, where there are many details that Matthew omits. (For instance, that those who brought the man reached Jesus through a hole in the roof of the house.)

Matthew leaves aside all of those details in order to underscore the central theme of the story: Jesus' power to forgive sins. In contrast to the other miracles in which Jesus heals the sick, in this case the first thing he does is to speak a word of forgiveness over the man who was paralyzed. Then, when the scribes comment that he is blaspheming, claiming for himself an authority which belongs only to God, Jesus confirms his words by healing the paralytic.

Opposition is growing. Matthew gave us a hint of that opposition at the very beginning of the Gospel in telling us about Herod's reaction when he learned of the birth of Jesus. But that was years ago, when Jesus had just been born. Now his ministry has been moving ahead with little opposition. The main enemies so far have been the demons, whom Jesus has cast out of sundry people. In the episode of the Gadarenes, which we studied yesterday, we see the beginning of opposition among those who see their own economic interest threatened.

In today's passage, it is the scribes (the most outstanding and serious students of Scripture) who begin speaking evil of Jesus. From this point on opposition will grow, slowly but inexorably, leading to the trial and crucifixion of Jesus.

Judge: Yesterday you began considering some evil or injustice that you would oppose in your community. You also decided to speak to others about it.

How have they responded to the issues you have raised? Have you encountered opposition or criticism? If you have had no such negative responses, do you expect them as you move on with your project?

The truth is that most good works and just causes encounter opposition because there is always someone who benefits from evil and injustice. Sometimes those who react negatively do so for economic reasons (like the owners of the swine) and sometimes for reasons of prestige and authority (like the scribes). But in both cases they are opposed to these works because they have something to lose. Frequently Christians are disheartened and surprised that the actions they take with the simple good intention of serving others can arouse such opposition. But good is always opposed.

Act: Return to what you resolved yesterday. Examine and consider all the possible sources of opposition. Think about how you will respond when such opposition materializes. Seek the help and support of others. Above all, offer yourself up once more in prayer and ask for God's guidance and strength.

Fourth Day: Read Matthew 9:9-13

6/5/05

See: Jesus calls another of his disciples, Matthew. (This is possibly the same Matthew after whom this Gospel is named.) Matthew was a tax collector. That is the meaning of the assertion that he was "sitting at the tax booth." These tax collectors, known as publicans, were not well regarded by the Jewish people. In the first place, they were agents of the Roman Empire, which held Israel in subjection. Second, many of them abused their power and exploited people. Third, the mere act of business transactions with Gentiles made them unclean before the eyes of the stricter Jews. In spite of all this, Jesus invites Matthew to follow him. The rest of the episode takes place in Matthew's home. (Although here the text says simply "in the house," Mark 2:15 tells us it was indeed the house of the tax collector.) There Jesus and his disciples are eating with "many tax collectors and sinners." That was to be expected. Since Matthew himself was a publican, this would mean that he would not have many friends among the people at large. Those who were there were Matthew's friends.

Then the Pharisees criticized Jesus for joining with such people. (Note the answer that Jesus gives in verses 12-13.)

Judge: Why do you think the Pharisees were upset at seeing Jesus eating with "tax collectors and sinners"? (Remember that the Pharisees were among the most religious people at the time. Their pride was that they obeyed the Law and kept themselves free of all uncleanness.)

Think again about what you have been considering during these last days, that is, the need to do some work of service or justice in your community. Among the objections that have been raised, has someone suggested that what you are proposing will involve either you or the church with unworthy people? What would Jesus reply to such objections?

Act: Write down in your notebook the words of Jesus in verse 12. Think about who the "well" are in your context (perhaps you, other believers, the leaders of the church, and so forth), and who the "sick" are (those whom you know you must help and invite, even though others may oppose it). Think about possible criticisms. Write them down. Ask God to give you the proper answer to such criticisms. Write down those answers. Confirm your resolve to become involved in your community for good and justice. Write down your resolution as a covenant between you, God, and the needy.

Fifth Day: Read Matthew 9:14-17

See: Criticism continues. Now it comes from a closer quarter: the disciples of John the Baptist. As we saw in the beginning of this study, there was always a close connection between Jesus and his disciples on the one hand and John and his on the other. After the death of John, his disciples did not disperse. On the contrary, as may be seen from this text and from other sources, for some time there still was within Judaism a movement composed of followers of John the Baptist. Those who now come to Jesus are people who feel a certain affinity with him but who are not his disciples. Their question is not necessarily malicious, as most of the ones the scribes and Pharisees pose. But it is still a familiar question in that they think the disciples of Jesus are not sufficiently religious, for they do not fast.

Jesus answers that since he is still among his disciples, for them this is still time for celebration, and not fasting. Then he offers them the words regarding a new patch on an old cloak and new wine (that is, unfermented juice) in old wineskins.

Judge: As modern readers, our first reaction would be to understand Jesus as telling us to get rid of everything that is old. This is because in the modern world it is quite common to think that whatever is new is necessarily better than the old. It certainly is true that many new things are better than the old. For instance, if we have to undergo surgery, it certainly is better to use modern anesthetics than to use the old methods. But there are also many cases when the old is better than the new, such as some family customs, traditional respect and courtesies, and so forth.

What Jesus means is not that one must reject everything that is old but that one must take care lest, in mixing the new with the old incorrectly, both the new wine and the old wineskins be lost. If each thing is put in its own place, "both are preserved."

Act: List the "old" things that should be kept, some of which you may have even neglected. (For instance, attending church regularly, respect for parents, devoting time for study and reflection, spending time in conversation with family, and others.) Make a list of some new things that now occupy your time. Reflect on how to keep the best of the old and, at the same time, make use of the new without having one destroy the other.

Ask yourself, *What do I have to do in order to keep the good both of the old and the new?*

Write down your reflections.

Sixth Day: Read Matthew 9:18-31

See: The passage includes three miracles. List them in your notebook: the daughter of the leader of the synagogue, the woman with hemorrhages, and the two blind men. You will see a common thread joining the three: Jesus touched each of these three people. For us, it is not as remarkable as it would have been for a Jew in the time of Jesus, for a religious person should not have touched any of these people.

The daughter of the leader of the synagogue was dead. To touch a dead body would render a person unclean, forcing a process of purification. However, Jesus takes her by the hand, and she rises.

The woman with hemorrhages was also considered unclean. This was thought of any menstruating or otherwise bleeding woman. Whoever would touch her would also be unclean until having submitted to a process of purification. But when Jesus discovers that the woman has touched him, he does not scold her, as would have been done by any other religious figure at that time, but rather encourages her and heals her.

Something similar happens with the two blind men, for a person was not supposed to touch any ailing part of the body. But Jesus touches their eyes and restores their sight.

Judge: Why do you think Jesus was willing to touch or to be touched by these people? What do you think the woman with hemorrhages thought when she realized that even though she had touched Jesus with her supposedly unclean body, he would not fault her for that?

Are there any "untouchables" in our society? Why do people shun them, as if any contact would contaminate them? What do you think Jesus would do were he to meet such a person today? What do you think Jesus would tell us about our shying away from such "untouchables" in our community?

Act: In your notebook, write down and complete the following phrase: *Today, or as soon as I can, I am going to approach* ————. *I will try to show (him or her) the love of Christ.*

Confess before God why you do not like that person. Ask for forgiveness and, above all, for a loving spirit.

Seventh Day: Read Matthew 9:32-38 6-12-05

See: Since today we shall devote a bit more time to biblical study, we can now consider a subject that has appeared before in the Gospel of Matthew but which we have not discussed yet: the theme of demons as causing disease. We encountered this theme already when discussing the Gadarene demoniacs. It now appears again in the case of the man who was mute and was brought before Jesus.

On reading this passage, our first thought is that it simply reflects a primitive mentality, which attributes disease to demons. Then we tell ourselves that today we know about germs and hormones, about genes and psychoses, and that therefore, there is no longer any need to speak of a connection between demons and disease. If someone is deaf, normally we do not say that he or she has a demon of deafness but rather that the auditory nerve has been damaged, or we give some other explanation. If someone does not behave rationally, we say that this person has a hormonal imbalance or that he or she has suffered a trauma. With that, we tell ourselves that we have already explained the origin of the disease.

All of these material, chemical, and scientific explanations are valid and important, but they do not go beyond an immediate and short-term explanation of the mechanism of evil. They explain the physical or chemical reason why a person has a certain disease but not the ultimate reason. Any true explanation would need to go beyond mere physical or chemical explanations. Let us consider an example:

A young man dies in a traffic accident. We visit his mother, and she asks us: "Why did my son die; he who was so good, so promising, so full of life?" It would be absurd and even cruel to respond to such a question by saying: "Because he had a fractured skull." Physically, that answer is correct. The young man died because during the traffic accident his skull was fractured, and there was a severe hemorrhage. But from the point of view of the bereaved mother, that is no answer; it is a physical explanation. What the mother really wishes to know is the ultimate reason of her son's death and her own suffering.

At that level, all that we can say is that we really don't know why her son died. We do know that death is bad; that the young man did not die because God killed him; that there are powers of evil in the world; that evil is most real and most far-reaching in that we cannot explain it. That is what the ancients meant when they spoke of "demons." Death and disease, even though we know that they might be the result of an infection or a skull fracture, are the work of the powers that oppose God.

If we then look at the case of a sick person who is healed, that healing is both a physical or chemical reality and a victory over the demon (a "casting out" of the demon).

Let us take the case of two people with hearing difficulties. The first one goes through surgery and is now able to hear. This has been accomplished by a surgeon. Yet, even though the surgeon might never use such terms—may even consider them ridiculous—what has taken place is a casting out of the demon of deafness. The other person is healed through prayer. That, too, is a victory over the demon of deafness. The latter is neither a greater victory or a lesser one because it has been achieved without medical intervention. It is a victory because the person can now hear, because the evil of deafness has been destroyed.

What this means is that when the Bible speaks of disease as the work of a demon, we do not have to choose between believing what the Bible says and what we are told by physicians and other scientists.

Continue reading the text, and you will see that matters become more complicated. In verse 34 we are told that the Pharisees said "by the ruler of the demons he casts out the demons." The power of evil is such that it even manages to make good appear evil. The Pharisees consider themselves good. They seek to obey the letter of the law in every detail. A few days ago, we saw some of the reasons they were prejudiced against Jesus. Now that prejudice leads them to judging falsely, deciding that the good that Jesus has done in healing the sick is not really good but is itself a work of the demon. This is a theme that we have encountered repeatedly during our reading of Matthew. The good is not always self-evident nor is it always accepted on its own authority.

In today's text, Jesus' action affects the prestige of the Pharisees, who claim to be more religious and better believers than Jesus himself. But Jesus can heal, and they cannot. The only way to explain such a situation is by claiming that the miracles which Jesus performs do not come from God but from the demon.

Verses 35-38 mark an important transition in the Gospel of Matthew. Up to this point, we have been studying about the teachings and ministry of Jesus. The disciples have appeared mostly as passive participants, whose task has been limited to following Jesus, listening to him, and occasionally asking a question. From this point on Jesus begins to prepare his disciples to continue his ministry. Were the Gospel of Matthew to end here, we could well believe that Jesus came, did much good, and then simply abandoned us.

But here we encounter a different reality: Jesus not only carried on his own ministry but also prepared and commissioned his disciples to continue it. In next week's studies we shall see more about this. But it is important for us to notice now the new direction which the Gospel of Matthew is beginning to take.

Note why Jesus will commission his disciples. Very often we want our own work to continue, want it to be completed by someone else. Such a desire is quite natural. But the reason that leads Jesus to commission his disciples to continue and expand his ministry is different. He is not concerned about himself or the continuation of his own work but rather for the needs of the people. Matthew tells us that "when he saw the crowds, he had compassion for them, because they were harassed and helpless, like sheep without a shepherd" (9:36). Jesus wishes his work to reach all. But the multitudes are too large—even without taking into consideration the thousands and thousands of other "cities and villages" beyond the horizon. That is why he says "the harvest is plentiful, but the laborers are few."

For understanding this last image, one must remember that when the grain of wheat is ripe, it must be harvested as soon as possible. Otherwise the harvest may be lost. The harvest will not wait for a time that is convenient to the harvester.

Judge: The text tells us that Jesus went about curing "every disease and every sickness." For your reflection on the text you just studied, consider the following question:

Are there diseases, problems, or difficulties that the church ignores and would rather not face?

Think about the following:

In the context of literal "sicknesses," sometimes it would seem that some are more worthy of compassion than others. For instance, whoever suffers from cancer can say it in the church and ask for the prayers of the faithful. When someone does this, the response is one of compassion. But there are churches in which if someone declares that he or she is suffering from AIDS, rather than showing the same compassion, they are excluded and even condemned. What do you think about this?

Then there are other diseases that are particularly stigmatized in some of our religious communities. That is the case, for instance, with alcoholism and other addictions. In such cases we convince ourselves that we do not have to have compassion for such people because, after all, it is their problem.

But Jesus never asked a sick person why he or she was sick before healing them. What is more, Jesus rejected the opinions of those who thought that when someone was sick, it was the result of a sin that had been committed either by that particular person or by his or her ancestors.

There are other "ills" that are not, strictly speaking, diseases but that are just as harmful, if not more. One of them is hunger. There are, today, many people who suffer hunger both in faraway and tragically impoverished countries and in the midst of our own relatively rich society. Hunger is also demonic. Later on we shall see Jesus dealing with this ill also and telling us to follow his example.

What do you think about hunger in our community? What are you doing to alleviate it?

One of the ways in which the demon acts against God's will is injustice, which sometimes results in disease. Think again, for instance, about hunger. How much of it is due to injustice? Then ask yourself: How is the demon of injustice acting in my own community? What can I do against that demon? What can the church do?

Act: Today's passage ends with a commandment: "Ask." That must be our first action in response to what we have just seen and judged: to ask the Lord of the harvest to send laborers to the harvest. But asking also implies acting in such a way that we ourselves are part of the response to what we ask. It is not a matter of asking God, from our comfortable pews, to send laborers, and then for us to remain comfortably seated waiting for those laborers to be somebody else. The commitment to "ask" implies the following three things:

1. Asking God for it. Do it.

2. Offering oneself as at least part of the answer. Think about all the needs around you (all the sorts of "harvests" that must be gathered) and offer yourself as a response to at least one of them: those who do not know the gospel and need a witness and an invitation; those who suffer from disease and need help and comfort; those who suffer from loneliness, anxiety, and other similar circumstances; and those who suffer from hunger, poverty, or injustice.

3. Inviting other people to offer themselves also as an answer to your prayer. Think about all the needs that have just been mentioned. Think about others whom you know, whose gifts make them particularly suitable to respond to any one of those needs. Write down on your notebook the names of those people and, by each name, a few words that remind you what kind of service you will invite them to consider. Pray for each person. During the next few days, speak at least once with each of them, asking for the guidance of the Holy Spirit both for you and for the other person. Do not try to force your views on them, but simply suggest the possibility that they may be called to a particular kind of service.

For Group Study

This study has two parts:

1. There is the question of a relationship between disease and the

demonic, as it appears under the heading of "See." As a discussion leader, make certain that all understand what is said about how speaking of "demons" in connection with disease or other forms of evil does not contradict medical science and is not an inferior or more primitive way of speaking about disease.

2. On the discussion about the "harvest" and how God calls different laborers to deal with various aspects of the "harvest," review with the group, and increase the list in the section "Act," where the meaning of "asking" is amplified. Write the resulting list on a blackboard or elsewhere for all to see.

Then allow each person who so wishes, to do one or both of the following:

1. To offer oneself as a response to that need. (For instance, if someone wishes to respond to the problem of hunger, that person may wish to offer to work as a volunteer in one of the various programs already existing in the community.)

2. To name a gift, quality, or talent that they have seen in someone else in the group, which could be an indication that God is inviting that other person to be part of the answer to the plea that the Lord of the harvest will send laborers to the harvest.

W E E K
FIVE

First Day: Read Matthew 10:1-15

See: Today's passage deals with the sending of the Twelve. On reading the text, what first strikes us is that Jesus is not sending them on an easy mission.

The first thing he tells them is that he is sending them only to "the house of Israel." This limit to the mission was provisional, for later Jesus would tell them that the time had come to go throughout the world.

What the disciples are to do among the people is heal the sick, raise the dead, cleanse the lepers, and cast out demons (verse 8).

Furthermore, they are not to expect payment for such services except that which is absolutely necessary for survival.

Nor are they to go armed with economic resources. They are to take no gold, silver, or even copper. They are not to take any money at all. Nor are they to take provisions on the road such as an extra tunic or sandals. Their procedure will be simply to arrive at a house, greet the people, and see how they receive them. If they do not welcome them or listen to them, they are to shake off the dust from their feet and to go elsewhere, leaving the punishment in God's hand.

Judge: As we read the entire New Testament, we see that some of the characteristics of this mission were temporary. For instance, we know that eventually Jesus told his disciples to go not only to the "house of Israel" but also "to all nations" (28:19). We also know that on another occasion Jesus told his disciples to take provisions with them (Luke 22:35-36).

Therefore, we do not have to apply this passage literally to all that we do today, as if Jesus had intended for his mission to be forever patterned after this first sending of the Twelve. But there are certain characteristics of this original sending which appear continuously throughout the

Christian mission. The most important of these is that it is a holistic mission. Jesus sends his disciples, and sends us, to preach and to heal, to announce the coming of God's reign, and to lead lives which prepare us for that reign.

When the church proclaims the gospel, it continues the work of Jesus. When the church heals the sick, feeds the hungry, or protects the weak, it is also continuing the ministry of Jesus.

Act: Think of that aspect of a holistic mission which you have most neglected. Write it down. Decide that during this week you will pay special attention to that aspect. Leave a blank space in your notebook so later, toward the end of the week, you may write down what you have done in this regard.

Second Day: Read Matthew 10:16-25

See: Today's passage is a continuation of yesterday's. Jesus goes on giving instructions to his disciples, who are now sent on their mission. He also tells them that this will not be easy.

It is interesting that here Jesus speaks to his disciples in terms of animals that were quite common in that place and time, such as sheep, wolves, snakes, and doves. The message is clear. There will be many enemies all around. Christians, without allowing themselves to be twisted by the malice of those enemies, must remember that they exist.

Jesus also mentions councils, synagogues, governors, and kings. All of those organizations and positions existed both in Palestine and in the nearby areas at the time of Jesus. Some were mostly religious in nature (councils and synagogues) while kings ruled with the blessing of Roman authorities, and governors were direct functionaries of the Roman Empire.

Judge: When reading the entire New Testament, it is apparent that the mission of early Christians was not easy. Sometimes we imagine this was so only in the early centuries and that over time it has become easier to be a Christian. But the truth is that whenever Christians have decided to be truly such, this has brought them difficulties, opposition, and even suffering. The reason is that as long as God's reign on earth is not fulfilled, human society will be organized on the basis of principles that are different from those of the reign, and anyone who seeks to live as a citizen of

God's reign, and especially to proclaim its principles, will necessarily clash with an existing order. Right now, in every country of the world, there are Christians who suffer because of their faith. Even in those countries where there is greatest freedom there are still Christians who suffer opposition from the general population and even from the government because they insist on protecting the rights of the poor, the exiled, and the marginalized.

Therefore, while we must be thankful that we do not live under regimes that are decidedly hostile to Christianity, we must also ask ourselves if part of the ease with which we are able to practice our faith might not be due to that faith having lost some of its flavor, so that the opposition or contrast between it and the values of the surrounding society is not really apparent.

If we were more faithful disciples, what sort of criticism or opposition would we find?

What would be the most likely sources of opposition or resistance?

Act: Pray for the wisdom and the strength to be more faithful. Invite others to join you in the same plea. Write down the answers God gives you.

Third Day: Read Matthew 10:26-33   6-19-05

See: Jesus is still giving the disciples instructions for their mission. In yesterday's text he warned them about the persecutions that they would have to face. Now he tells them that, in spite of all such difficulties, they are not to be afraid. There are several reasons for this:

What is now covered will be uncovered. This means that God's reign, which the disciples are proclaiming and which is still hidden, will eventually be made manifest.

Those enemies who kill the body are not the most dangerous. The most dangerous are those who destroy both the body and the soul.

God watches over the disciples, whose hairs are counted and who are of more value than the birds, for which God also cares.

Finally, the last point returns to the first: Whoever acknowledges Jesus in public will be acknowledged by Jesus before the Father, and whoever denies him will also be denied.

Judge: During the last few days we have seen that the mission to which Jesus sends us as "laborers in the harvest" is not easy and may even lead to persecution. Now we come to the natural consequence of those possible difficulties: fear.

Fear is not only a consequence of such difficulties but can also be a cause for disobedience. We have been reflecting on what we are to do in order to be obedient to the Lord. We have spoken of the difficulties that true obedience may produce. Now we face a harsh truth: If we are disobedient, very often it is out of fear. It is out of fear of rejection that we remain silent when there is an opportunity for witness. It is for fear of losing our employment that we do not protest against injustice in the workplace. It is for fear of public opinion that we allow ourselves to be carried by the current, even though we know that it is headed in the wrong direction.

Act: Remember a particular situation in which fear led you either to act or not to act. While thinking of that situation, read the passage in Matthew again. That fear which leads to disobedience, is it not lack of faith?

Write in your notebook a brief account of what happened in that situation and how you acted. Write another account of what you should have done. Pray, asking for forgiveness for the first and for strength for the second.

Fourth Day: Read Matthew 10:34-42

See: Verses 34-39 present a series of contrasts, some of them rather unexpected. Since we have heard these verses before, perhaps they do not surprise us. But try to read them as if it were the first time. The first contrast is between "peace" and the "sword." Since we know the general outline of the message of Jesus, we would expect him to tell us he came to bring peace, and in a way, that is precisely what he came for. But here he tells us that he came to bring "a sword." Likewise, we would expect Jesus to defend what we call "family values." But Jesus tells us that if we love family more than him we are not worthy of him.

The reason for this is all that we have seen in recent days: The message of Jesus leads to conflict and even persecution. If we think otherwise, we fool ourselves, and we do not know how powerful evil really is. The result of all this is a striking paradox: Those who find their own life lose it, and those who lose their own life find it.

Then the passage seems to change in tone suddenly. After speaking about difficulties and rejection, it speaks of acceptance, of receiving, of giving cups of cold water.

Judge: Why do you think Jesus says that he did not come to bring peace, but a sword? Do you know of any cases in which this may be clearly seen? (For instance, a young man who decided to join the church, and this led to difficulties with his family. Or a woman who decided that she was being called to the ordained ministry, and this produced tensions within her own marriage.)

Think then about the conflicts that the early Christians had with the Roman Empire, to the point that many of them died as martyrs. Although these people found in the gospel a profound peace, it also literally brought to them the sword and death.

Even after all this talk about rejection, strife, and the sword, Jesus speaks about acceptance, receiving, and giving a cup of cold water. Christians are to be known not because they are constantly looking for enemies or because they are in a sour mood but rather because they give water when others do not and because they receive those whom others reject.

Note above all that, after speaking about such dramatic things as persecution and death, Jesus ends his speech referring to a cup of cold water. Sometimes the greatest things are seemingly minor ones.

Act: Read verse 42 once more. Think about a cup of cold water. There is nothing heroic about giving someone a bit of water, but still it is an act of obedience. Before being faithful in the great and heroic, one has to be faithful in the seemingly small. Look about you and think of small acts of love and service that you may perform without having to await the moment that may require heroic obedience.

Fifth Day: Read Matthew 11:1-19

See: Once again we find the matter of the relationship between John and his disciples on the one hand and Jesus and his on the other. Here we are told that John is still in prison and hears about the deeds of Jesus. What John hears about Jesus is precisely what was expected of the Messiah, or the Christ. In order to make certain that Jesus is truly the Messiah, John sends two of his disciples to ask him. Rather than responding directly Jesus points to what is happening. It is not a matter of words nor of his claiming a particular title for himself. It is rather a matter of facts such as that the blind see, the lame walk, and the deaf hear.

Jesus takes the opportunity to refer to John and his own ministry with very positive words: "Among those born of women no one has arisen greater than John the Baptist" (verse 11). He also comments that there are those who will receive neither him, nor John the Baptist. The latter led an austere life, and he was criticized and rejected for his austerity. Jesus eats and drinks with common folk, and they reject him because they think that he is a glutton and a drunkard.

Judge: After responding to John's disciples and affirming the ministry of the Baptist, Jesus comments about those who now reject him saying that he is a glutton and a drunkard but earlier rejected John because he was too austere. If John goes to the desert, dresses with camel's hair, and eats locusts and honey, he must be mad. If Jesus remains in the cities, eating and drinking with the people in them, they say that he is a glutton and a drunkard. In point of fact, they simply do not wish to listen to the word of God and will always find an excuse.

Do you know of anyone who always finds an excuse not to hear the word of God? Do you ever find yourself in such a situation?

Act: Acknowledge that God acts in people who lead ascetic lives and also in those who eat and drink. Think about someone whom you know who leads an austere life and resolve to imitate that person's commitment. Think of someone else who "eats and drinks," and resolve to imitate that person's joy and accessibility. Try to combine both.

Sixth Day: Read Matthew 11:20-24

See: This passage is often called the "woes to unrepentant cities." Here Jesus refers to cities in which he himself has walked, preached, and performed miracles. They are all cities whose inhabitants consider themselves to be good and faithful Jews. He compares them with pagan and unforgiving cities and says that their punishment will be worse than the punishment of those other cities.

In order to understand the power of what Jesus is saying, we must place ourselves at the time when these words were spoken. Tyre and Sidon were two of the most important Phoenician cities (that is, they were Philistine towns). They were traditional enemies of Israel and its God. The story of Sodom is well known. Sodom was the city that God destroyed because rather than practicing hospitality it sought to violate God's envoys.

Now Jesus compares those cities of terrible histories with three supposedly believing cities and declares that judgment upon the latter three will be worse than the judgment that will befall the proverbial cruel, pagan, and disbelieving cities.

Judge: Here we find a theme that is quite common throughout the Gospels. Those who think themselves to be privileged because they are religious are at risk of falling into even greater sin than others. The opposite is also true: Sinners, tax collectors, and prostitutes will enter the reign of God ahead of the religious scribes and Pharisees. This will be so, not because their sin is not real but precisely because they know themselves to be sinners and therefore will repent, whereas those who think themselves "holy" and "pure" will not repent. Here Jesus says the same thing, although speaking about cities rather than about individuals.

Have you ever thought it possible that some of the people who consider themselves most religious may be further from God and God's forgiveness than those who know that they are sinners?

Act: Since you have decided to subject yourself to the discipline of these studies, you are most likely a religious person. In that sense, you and I are closer to the scribes and Pharisees than to publicans and sinners and closer to Chorazin than to Tyre. We are believers. We want to be faithful. But even here there is a danger. If we do not learn to repent as the worst of sinners, we shall find ourselves far from the reign of God.

Write the following on your notebook: *Sinners, of which I am the first.* Remember some of the many reasons you have for writing such words. Confess your sins to God, repent, and ask for newness of life.

Seventh Day: Read Matthew 11:25-30   7-3 ⁻ᵒⁿ⁵

See: During this week we have been studying what Jesus told his disciples as he sent them on his mission. In this study, we have encountered some harsh words from Jesus about what following him really means. First, he requires those followers to take with them no provisions. Then he tells them that he is sending them "like sheep into the midst of wolves," and that they will suffer persecution (10:16). He warns them that "in the synagogues," that is, in the most religious places, they will be flogged. He adds that "brother will betray brother to death"; that he has not come to bring peace, but a sword; that anyone who loves father or mother more than him is not worthy of him; that one has to take up the cross and lose one's life.

Yesterday, we saw Jesus pronouncing a more severe judgment on the unrepentant religious cities than over the pagan and immoral cities of Tyre, Sidon, and Sodom. Now the tone will change radically, for Jesus will speak about infants, about being gentle and humble, and above all about resting.

Verse 24 serves as a bridge between yesterday's passage and today's. Yesterday, Jesus seemed to overturn the order of judgment on the cities: Instead of thinking of a greater condemnation for those that are further from God, he spoke of such condemnation for those that are near. Here, Jesus once again overturns the expected order. One would expect for "the wise and the intelligent" to be able to penetrate the mysteries of God better than others. But here Jesus says exactly the opposite: God has hidden these things from the wise and intelligent and has revealed them to infants.

While there is a parallelism between these passages, there is also a contrast. Yesterday's passage spoke about cities and about the judgment of heaven. Upon reading it, no doubt we remembered the judgment upon Sodom and Gomorrah. Today things seem less dramatic, more peaceful. It is a matter of the wisdom of infants. (In a way, this contrast reminds us of what we saw three days ago when, after speaking about the need for a heroic obedience, Jesus ended his speech by referring to a cup of cold water given to the thirsty.)

At this point we have moved from the spectacular to the quiet, from the far-reaching and severe judgment on cities to the affirmation of the wisdom of infants. This sets the tone for the entire passage: one of movement from risk to affirmation. Before, Jesus was speaking of heroic obedience and of how difficult it is to follow him. Now he speaks of a light burden and an easy yoke. The center of the entire passage is the invitation, which we have so often heard with great joy: "Come to me, all you that are weary and are carrying heavy burdens, and I will give you rest" (verse 28).

Whoever has read only the earlier passage, with its announcements of persecution and its call to losing one's life and to heroic obedience, might think that this is all that Jesus asks of us: a heroic obedience, a life of constant sacrifice. But that is only one side of the coin.

The other side appears in today's passage: What we are to do is not so difficult, for it has been revealed to babes. What we have to do is not so heavy, for the yoke is easy. We have no need to be anxious and tense, for the Lord invites us to come to him for rest.

Judge: During the last few days we have been studying texts that call us to a difficult sort of obedience. If we had studied only those texts, we could easily think Christian faith is a matter of long faces and harsh customs. Throughout history there have been many Christians who have believed this. On the basis of that understanding of the Christian faith, some have dressed in rags and moved to dwell in the desert, punishing their body with exaggerated fasting and other similar practices. Others have established strict rules of conduct, making long lists of what Christians are not to do, and have then set out to supervise other people's lives in order to make certain that they are true Christians.

However, one does not have to go to such extremes to find Christians who believe that all faith must be heroic, or it is not faith. These are usually sad-faced Christians. For them, faith is a matter of anxiety; instead of offering them rest, it becomes a heavy yoke. Because the burden is heavy, they also tend to impose it on others, telling them that if they do not lead dry and austere lives, they are not true Christians.

There is certainly a heroic aspect to the Christian faith. In extreme circumstances, whoever claims to be a disciple of Jesus must be ready to surrender life for him. That is why we admire the martyrs of the first century, missionaries such as David Livingstone and Albert Schweitzer, leaders such as Martin Luther King, Jr., and Caesar Chavez, and people such as Mother Teresa. Furthermore, there are many people whose faith is heroic but who never become famous.

Do you know someone whose life is of true holiness without announcements and fanfare? Someone who quietly gives a significant part of his or her income to support the work of the church and a number of just causes without expecting any kind of gratitude? Someone who spends long hours in prayer, interceding for the needy and bereaved? Someone who spends days off visiting the sick in hospitals? Throughout my life, I have known many such people.

But that is only one of the two faces of faith. The other face is having true faith such that our burdens are no longer ours. That is why Jesus invites us to come to him and find rest. The reason all of these aforementioned people have been able to have truly heroic faith is that their faith is not a burden. It is faith that truly rests in Jesus.

Whoever tries to lead a life of heroic dimensions without having child-like faith, resting in Jesus, will become an empty and harried Christian and, therefore, a false Christian. For such Christians, the yoke is not easy nor is the burden light.

Act: Today we complete our first five weeks with Matthew. We said at the beginning that this study, as any other, would require discipline. But we also said that such discipline, which at first may seem forced and even difficult, would progressively become easier and perhaps necessary. In the introduction, we compared this discipline to exercise, which at first needs much willpower and effort but slowly becomes a custom and a need so that whoever is used to exercising and does not, feels that something is missing. But in truth this sort of discipline goes beyond that of physical exercise. This discipline should become pleasant for us because it should lead us to an ever-deeper faith, a faith that increasingly learns to rest more on Jesus and less on itself.

Think for a few minutes about your discipline of study and how it has evolved during the last five weeks. Has it become easier and more pleasant? If so, give thanks to God. Is it still a burden, a routine that is difficult to maintain? In that case, ask God to increase your faith and to allow you to savor the delights of the divine presence so that you may better and more clearly experience the joy of coming to Jesus Christ and finding rest in him.

Naturally, all of this does not diminish the reality of what we have been studying in recent days: that faith may well lead to serious difficulties and even to persecution and death. All of that is still true. But it seems different when it takes place within the context of a faith that does not trust in its own achievement nor even in its obedience, but in Jesus Christ.

Spend a few minutes in absolutely silent prayer. By absolutely, I mean a prayer in which you say nothing, ask for nothing—not even silently. Not even in your innermost heart. Say no word. Ask for nothing. Simply remain there in God's presence. Rest. Forget your anxieties. Forget even your holiest concerns. If they keep coming to your mind, simply pass them over to God.

Rest. If you get sleepy, do not be concerned. Sleep in the presence of God as you would in the presence of a friend or a loved one. When you feel that God's presence fills your soul, open your eyes. Look around you, but now look at the world in God's company. See if you have not experienced something of what Jesus meant when he said "come to me, all you that are weary and are carrying heavy burdens, and I will give you rest."

Write in your notebook a few words about how you feel after this experience of prayer.

For Group Study

Review with the entire group what we have been studying beginning with Matthew 9:35. Write on a large sheet of paper: *The cost of discipleship.* Under those words, as the group summarizes what we have been studying, make a list of what Jesus told his disciples would be the cost of their discipleship.

After making that list, write another heading next to the first: *The reason for our calling.* Ask the group to look again at Matthew 9:36-38, where they will see that the reason for our calling is compassion for the multitudes.

Begin a third column with the heading: *Rewards of discipleship.* Now read Matthew 10:40-42 and 11:28-30. Point out that the entire passage begins with words of comfort and compassion and that, at its very center, we find a glimpse of the rewards of discipleship (Matthew 10:40-42).

Now divide the group into two subgroups. Tell them that there will be a debate. One band will defend the proposition: *True faith is heroic.* The other side will defend the proposition: *True faith is simple, joyful, and restful.* Tell each side that they must base all their arguments on Matthew 9:35–11:30. Give them a few minutes to prepare. Then, let two or three people from each side have three minutes each to expound and defend their position. After the debate, bring the group together again and show how the two positions are two sides of the same coin.

You may end the session with a short discussion on the sort of prayer suggested in the previous section. After such a discussion, ask all to sit in a circle and to approach God in absolute silence. After some time of silent prayer, close the session by simply saying out loud: *Amen!*

W E E K
SIX

First Day: Read Matthew 12:1-8

See: It is interesting to note that in yesterday's passage Jesus promises rest to his followers, and that in today's passage the central theme is the day of rest. The events take place on the Sabbath, the day of rest. The rhythm of six days of work and one of rest is central to the law of Israel.

Jesus and his disciples are hungry, and they begin taking grain from the field to eat. From today's perspective, the fault we would find with such an action is that they seem to be stealing grain from someone else's field. But the law established that hungry travelers as well as the poor had the right to take food from the fields. They could not carry it away in order to sell it, which would indeed be theft, but they could eat what they needed.

Therefore, it is not a possible theft that disturbs the Pharisees but rather that Jesus and his disciples are breaking the law that commands rest on the Sabbath. They could have performed the same act any other day of the week without raising any eyebrows. But today is the Sabbath, and one must rest. Jesus responds by showing them that there are occasions and situations in which the law of rest must give way to other principles: When he was hungry, David ate what he was not supposed to eat; the priests in the Temple must work on the Sabbath day.

Judge: Today's text presents a conflict between two principles. On the one hand, the law says that one must rest on the Sabbath. On the other hand, God desires that those who are hungry have something to eat. The Pharisees insist on keeping the Sabbath even if this means that Jesus and his disciples must go hungry. Jesus responds by explaining that there are other situations that may take precedence over the law of the Sabbath.

The manner in which Jesus solves this conflict between two laws is by looking at the human need that requires a response. That is why he quotes, "I desire mercy and not sacrifice" (verse 7). Sacrifice was a religious practice ordered by the law and supervised by the priests. Mercy is compassion toward those in need. When religious practice and mercy seem to clash, one must opt for the latter.

We in the church have also been taught a number of rules. These rules are good, as the law of rest on the Sabbath is also good. But they must not be placed before human need.

Act: Consider the possibility that some aspects of your religion might be like that of the Pharisees, who are more concerned for rules than for human needs. Ask God to let you see clearly the meaning of the words of Jesus: "I desire mercy and not sacrifice."

Second Day: Read Matthew 12:9-21

See: The first part of today's passage is parallel to yesterday's text: Here we have another conflict regarding the Sabbath day. In this case the setting is not the fields but the synagogue. This means that we are now in the strictly religious sphere, where the Pharisees traditionally claim most authority. Now, in that religious atmosphere, they ask Jesus a tricky question, the purpose of which is to accuse him of not respecting the Sabbath.

Jesus responds in two ways: First, he points out that any of them would go and pull their sheep from a pit, even if this happened on a Sabbath. Therefore, they themselves do not obey the law as strictly as they claim. Second, Jesus shows them his love toward the man with the withered hand, as well as his own authority, by healing him. Jesus' response—both in word and in action—leaves the Pharisees with nothing to say, and they begin seeking a different way to destroy Jesus.

Judge: The Pharisees were quite ready to insist that all should keep the Sabbath. Still, if there was a conflict between that law and their own interests, they themselves would opt for the latter. Do we do the same?

The truth is that quite often we are ready to believe that our excuses and reasons for doing something are acceptable, but those which other people offer are not. If, for instance, we do not give the needy what they require, we can always convince ourselves that we do not have enough for our own needs. But if someone else says the same, we doubt it. If one day we do not attend church, we always have good reasons. But if someone else is not there, we question their faith and commitment.

Worst of all, if someone through either word or action shows or tells us that our excuses are not valid, we are quite likely to turn in judgment against that person—much like the Pharisees, who begin planning a way to destroy Jesus.

Act: Think of someone about whom you have thought ill during this last week. Think about your own actions and consider the possibility that you may have judged yourself with greater mercy or latitude than you are granting the other person.

Write down in your notebook, *I desire mercy and not sacrifice.* Ask God to help you look on other people with mercy, and act toward them with love, rather than with legalisms and condemnations.

Still in this period of prayer, think about those cases in which you have preferred to look on others with legalistic demands rather than with mercy. Every time you can think of one such case, write once again: *I desire mercy and not sacrifice.*

Third Day: Read Matthew 12:22-37

See: The polemic with the Pharisees continues. Note that, although the passage begins with a healing miracle, Matthew uses that narrative as an introduction to an entire series of Jesus' responses to the Pharisees. The occasion for this polemic is that "all the crowds" (that is, the vast numbers who have not made a commitment with or against Jesus) are amazed, and begin considering the possibility that Jesus may indeed be the Messiah.

The Pharisees have reason to be worried when they see people responding this way. In the first place, the popularity and increasing authority of Jesus detract from theirs. Furthermore, there are strong political reasons that must be understood in order to be fully aware of the roots of the attitude of the Pharisees toward Jesus. Although the Pharisees were not collaborators with the Roman regime, they had at least reached a compromise that allowed them to conserve their religion and their customs without having to submit to the idolatric practices of the Romans. But if the word began circulating among Jews that the Messiah had come, and this were to result in a strong nationalist movement, it was quite possible that the Romans would destroy what little freedom the Jews still had (which is in fact what happened a few years later). Therefore, when the Pharisees hear the crowds considering the possibility that Jesus may be the Son of David, or the Messiah, they have reason to be concerned.

Judge: There are many elements in the passage that are worthy of discussion and study, but center your attention on the Pharisees and their attitude. During these days of study, you have been invited in the name of Jesus to undertake a series of adventures of obedience, love, and service. Have you encountered criticism or opposition when you have tried to live out your decisions? Consider the possibility that these may not be personal criticism as much as they are expressions of fear similar to the fear of the Pharisees: fear of losing leadership and fear of changes which may involve risks and difficulties. Perhaps understanding the deeper dimensions of any opposition you encounter will help you know how to respond to it.

Act: Think now about your own answers to the calls from Jesus which you have heard during this study. If you hesitate, could there be something akin to the fears of the Pharisees? Consider the following:

The Pharisees feared for their prestige. Are you afraid of public opinion?

The Pharisees feared that the teachings of Jesus would challenge the established order in which they were relatively at ease. When Jesus calls you to a new act of obedience, do you hesitate out of fear that the manner in which you have ordered your life may be interrupted?

Fourth Day: Read Matthew 12:38-45

See: Once again, it is "some of the scribes and Pharisees" who ask Jesus for a "sign." The request itself is ridiculous and shows the incredulity of those who make it. We have seen Jesus repeatedly offering signs and miracles. Whoever does not believe, does so because of willful resistance and not because there have not been enough signs.

Jesus responds by telling them that the only sign that they will receive is "the sign of the prophet Jonah." This sign has two dimensions:

1. The three days and three nights in the belly of the sea monster.
2. The repentance of the people of Nineveh.

In a way, it is this second sign that infuriates the scribes and the Pharisees. Note that in Jonah's time it was the Ninevites who repented, and in Solomon's time the "queen of the South" came from a faraway country. Therefore, the "sign of Jonah" in this second sense is showing that people who were not supposed to be religious repented and believed, whereas the opposite is the case for the supposedly religious.

Judge: Look again at verses 39-42. Why do you think Jesus reminds the scribes and Pharisees of the repentance of Nineveh and the episode about the "queen of the South"? Could it be that he is reminding them that religious people must be careful lest they take their relationship with God for granted, as if they no longer needed faith and repentance?

Now read verses 43-45. What does Jesus mean by "the unclean spirit" that leaves a person but returns with even more spirits that are even more evil? Could it mean the same as the previous verses, for example, if religious people sweep and adorn their houses (that is, their lives), but leave them unoccupied, they become even more susceptible to the powers of evil? Is that not the great temptation of the scribes and Pharisees, for whom it is so difficult to repent and accept Jesus precisely because they are religious people? Could that also be one of our worst temptations?

Act: Spend a few minutes in a period of absolute silence such as you began practicing a few days ago. Wait until you feel you are in God's presence. Then, still in a spirit of prayer, open your notebook and read some of the decisions you have made in the days past. Every time you come across one you have not continued or fulfilled, ask God for forgiveness and strength. Think about the people whom you have seen doing what you had proposed to do, even though they may not have made a conscious decision such as yours. (For instance, if you made a resolution to forgive and saw somebody else forgiving, or if you had decided to help someone in need and saw someone else doing it while you did not.) Thank God for those people. Return to a prayer of absolute silence.

Fifth Day: Read Matthew 12:46-50

See: This is one of the harshest and most surprising passages in the entire Gospel of Matthew, for we usually think that Jesus must have been an exemplary son and brother. Here he seems not to acknowledge his own mother and brothers. However, Jesus does not say that Mary is not his mother or that his brothers are not such. He rather extends the bonds of family beyond those of birth. He says that those who listen to him and do the will of God are his "brother and sister and mother."

Judge: Do you see any connection between this passage and the one we studied yesterday? In both cases, there are people who would seem to belong to the "inner circle" around God or Jesus. In Israel, the scribes and

Pharisees certainly would seem to belong to God's inner circle. In this passage today, we would expect the mother and brothers of Jesus to be part of his inner circle, of those closest to him. But in both cases Jesus says that there is no such inner circle: Those who think that they are inside should take care lest they find themselves outside; and those who seem to be far away, can simply repent and do the will of God, and they will be as close as his mother and his brothers.

Is there an inner circle in your church? Do you belong to it? The church certainly needs leaders who direct and make its plans; but if those leaders believe that they are part of God's inner circle simply because of their leadership, it is time to warn them!

The opposite is also true. Place yourself in the situation of those who were listening to Jesus and who now hear that they are his brothers, sisters, and mother. If you think you are far away, you are probably much closer than you believe. All that you have to do is repent and lead a new life.

Act: If there is an inner circle in your church of which you are a part and if some of its members are following this study with you, discuss with them how the circle can be opened, inviting all to be part of the family of Jesus.

On the other hand, it is possible that you may feel that you are far from God. Perhaps you are new in the church and feel that you have much to learn. Perhaps you realize that your life is not as holy as it should be. In such a case, it is not a matter for despair but rather for repentance. Listen to the divine voice that calls you, *my sister, my brother,* and trust God.

Sixth Day: Read Matthew 13:1-9, 18-23 η–/0–0S

See: For today's reading, we have skipped verses 10-17, to which we shall return tomorrow. We will thus be able to study the Parable of the Sower as a whole, without dividing it into two days. Note that the explanation of the parable (verses 18-23) is given to the disciples and not to "the whole crowd" who stood on the beach and heard the parable itself. Tomorrow we shall discuss this further.

In the parable itself, the seed falls on four different places, which Jesus then explains as follows:

1. On the path. These are those who hear the word of God's reign but do not understand it. It is a seed that does not even germinate.

2. On rocky ground. Such seed sprouts soon because the rocks are warm, but it also dries soon. Such is the soil of those who receive the word with joy but without depth. When difficulties arise (in this case the sun), they forget what they have received.

3. Among thorns. These people listen to the word and receive it, but their concern over wealth chokes the crop.

4. On good soil. The seed gives fruit in abundant, and even shocking, proportions.

Judge: Although this is usually called the Parable of the Sower, the parable is really not about the sower or his sowing but rather about the seed and the various sorts of soil on which it falls. The subject of the parable is how to listen and how to respond.

The parable does not mean that some of us are always like rocky soil and others like good soil. Sometimes we respond like rocky soil and other times like good soil; sometimes we listen and obey, sometimes we listen and do not obey; and sometimes we do not listen or obey.

Think, therefore, of the parable, not in terms of the nonbelievers to whom you are to speak but in terms of yourself and what sort of soil you have been for the seed of the word.

Act: Jot down in your notebook, one under the other, the four types of soil mentioned in the parable. Then review your notebook and try to determine which type of soil you responded to on certain occasions. In your notebook, next to each of the four types, write down your reflections.

Pray God to make you fertile soil where God's word may grow and bear good and abundant fruit.

Seventh Day: Read Matthew 13:10-17

See: Remember that yesterday we studied the Parable of the Sower, which appears before today's text and is explained after it. That is why, even though yesterday we reached verse 23, today we return to verses 10-17.

Note the difference between verse 2, where we are told Jesus is speaking to "the whole crowd," and verse 10, where the question is posed by the disciples in private. The parable itself is addressed to the public at large, but the commentary about the parables in general, and the explanation of this particular one, is addressed only to the disciples.

Note also that, in opposition to what we are often told, the parables do not always serve to clarify what is being said. In this particular case, Jesus says that he speaks in parables to the crowd because "to you it has been given to know the secrets of the kingdom of heaven, but to them it has not been given." Later on, in verse 34, you will come across the same point: "Jesus told the crowds all these things in parables; without a parable he told them nothing."

What this means is that a parable is not a mere illustration that Jesus uses to clarify his teachings. On the contrary, sometimes the parables are means whereby Jesus is able to say something very harsh—something so harsh that were he to declare it openly it would cause an overwhelmingly negative reaction. Such is the case, for instance, of the many parables by which Jesus warns religious people that they should not think that because they are religious they are better than the rest or that they have an assurance of heaven. Such is the case also of many of the parables we shall be studying in weeks to come.

Most of the parables of Jesus are narratives, the purpose of which is to ensure that those who listen will suddenly find themselves faced with the message of God's reign. In many of them, the one whom we would expect to be the hero or protagonist turns out not to be such. Others show that sometimes things and people that seem to be of least value deserve greater attention. Many of them surprise us. In this they are similar to the famous parable in which Nathan told David about the man who had many sheep (see 2 Samuel 12:1-12).

Some of the parables of Jesus are allegories, that is, narratives in which each of the various elements has a figurative meaning. Such is the case of the Parable of the Sower, which Jesus explains making it clear that the seed is the preaching of God's reign. Each of the places where the seed falls also represents something in particular.

But even in the case of allegories we must take care lest we simplify the parable too much. For instance, yesterday we saw that the various sorts of places where the seed fell represent either various sorts of people or, even better, different attitudes that we take.

That interpretation is certainly valid and very helpful. But when we look at the parable with greater care, we see that it is also possible to read the parable in the sense that some *people* are sown in rocky ground, others on the path, others among thorns, and others in good soil. (Read verses 19-23 carefully, and you will see this.)

This may help us better understand the relationship between the parable and the explanation to the disciples in today's passage. The parable says that according to where each person is planted so will the seed planted in them vary in its fruit. Some people are "on the path," on hard ground, where the seed cannot even sprout. Others are "on rocky ground," where it is not possible to lay down roots and prosper. Others, among thorns, where other interests compete with the good seed in such a way that they finally smother it. And others are "in good soil" where they can give abundant fruit. In explaining to the disciples why he speaks to the multitudes in parables, Jesus tells them that it is because the crowds are not ready to understand the mysteries of God's reign. That is, they are people on the path, in rocky ground, or among thorns, so that whatever is sown in them will not bear fruit. In contrast, the disciples are in good soil, and therefore, Jesus speaks clearly to them so that they may bear more fruit. That is the meaning of verse 12.

This needs some clarification. In the introduction to this series of studies we saw that true Bible study requires discipline. If we do not delve deep into Scripture, if we do not allow it to delve deep within us, we should not expect to be able to read the Bible and suddenly understand everything. It is necessary for Scripture to mold our character, to shape our lives, so that we can understand Scripture and its meaning. Back to the example of the discipline of physical exercise, whoever wishes to be able to lift a very heavy weight must exercise constantly with lesser weights, which will be increased a little at a time. If one does not do this, when attempting suddenly to lift a great weight one will be injured. Likewise, those who insist on remaining "on the path" where there is no fertile soil should not expect the same fruit as those who move toward good soil. Thus, the disciples, who have abandoned their nets and their tax-collector benches in order to follow Jesus, are ready to hear his teachings and to understand them more clearly, while the crowds who come to listen out of curiosity and sit on the beach will only hear parables inviting them to approach the "good soil."

For those who do not seek to lay down roots in the good soil, the prophecy cited in verse 14 becomes true. After reading that verse, read today's passage again, and see if now you understand it better. Then read once again the entire parable of the sower (verses 1-23).

Judge: Note that there is a progression from one sort of soil to the other:

The area "on the path" is soil so hard that it is like stone. The seed cannot even be protected from the birds. Therefore, the parable doesn't even say that such seed sprouted.

The rocky ground is a bit more hospitable. Among the rocks, and perhaps in a thin layer above them, there is a bit of soil. That soil allows the seed to sprout. Furthermore, sometimes that seed even sprouts sooner because the stones radiate warmth. But when the seed begins to develop roots, it finds no depth, and the plant withers.

The soil where the thorns grow seems to be even more fertile than the good soil because there is abundant growth. Therefore, anyone who cannot distinguish between thorns and a proper crop will think that this is a very productive area. But eventually the thorns overpower the good seed and choke the plants.

Finally, there is the good soil, which is the only place where the seed can yield abundant fruit.

Think now about the various "places" where it is possible for you to try to "plant" your own life.

Some people prefer to stay "on the path," where it is not necessary to lay down roots nor to be committed to anything. Life on the path is interesting and fun. Along the path come all sorts of people. If I remain there, I can see and enjoy all of it without having to make any commitment. Time passes away; life is interesting; and I have no need to decide who I am or what I am to be.

These are the people who hear the gospel and pay little attention, for they find it boring because they are so used to the lights and the noises of the path that everything else seems dull. If they listen to someone who preaches, they do so out of curiosity, or because they like the music, or because there is nothing interesting to do. The truth is that they do not listen, but only watch, just as they would watch a ball game.

However, life on the path is not life. Time passes, and life leads nowhere. The seed does not sprout and eventually, as Jesus says, the birds of evil devour it.

Then, there are those who like the rocky ground. Like the path, the rocky ground has the attraction that it does not seem to demand much from us. The sower will not go looking for a harvest in the rocky ground, even though there exists on such ground a certain imitation of life. On rocky ground seeds do sprout and grow. As long as there is no sun or drought, they will even be lush. On rocky ground, I can become enthusiastic about something, and I can even make believe that I am committed;

but such commitment is as superficial as the soil. On rocky ground, I believe that I am alive, but still life leads nowhere.

There are many "rocky ground" Christians. They become enthused over eloquent preaching of the gospel. They raise their hand or go to the altar every time they are called to repentance, but then they forget their decision. They offer themselves as volunteers and then don't show up. When difficulty arises, they disappear. They are converted every day but never grow.

Third, there are those who are content living among thorns. Life among thorns seems interesting and sometimes even heroic. The little plant sprouts and is immediately surrounded by formidable opponents. Sometimes, the thorns even protect it from the birds and from the burning sun. But eventually the thorns will win, and the good seed will be choked.

Jesus declares clearly that these thorns are: "the cares of the world and the lure of wealth" (verse 22). I live among thorns when I convince myself that I can be a planting of Jesus Christ and at the same time be anxious about the cares of this world and about wealth. This is a great temptation, for all of society around me tells me that success in life consists precisely of acquiring fame and wealth.

The most fertile grounds, according to the wisdom of the world, are those where thorns abound: the circles of high society and high finances, the halls of success and of fame. There are even some Christians who think that being admitted into such circles is a sign of faithfulness to God and of divine blessing. But eventually the thorns choke the good seed. All our good intentions and our dreams of being faithful and fruitful Christians falter before the pressures of society, the quest for success, and the deceit of wealth.

Finally, there is the good soil. Strictly speaking, the good soil is no other than Jesus Christ, for it is only in him that we can really grow and bear fruit. If I wish to be a seed planted in good soil, I have no other option but to lay out my roots in Jesus Christ. Neither the path, nor the rocky soil, nor the seemingly apparent fertile area where thorns grow, can give me the depth of root necessary to bear fruit. It is only being "in Christ" that I will have life abundant.

Where is your life planted?

Act: Thankfully, the parable does not mean that whoever is on the path has no other option but to wait for the birds to come and devour his or her life. On the contrary, the Gospel throughout tells us repeatedly that there is an opportunity for repentance and newness of life. Thus, it is not simply a matter of analyzing the situation and discovering where we are, in order then to be reconciled with our lot. It is rather a matter of seeing where we are, in order then to decide where we should be.

If you are "on the path," and you spend all the time contemplating life—especially the life of others—without commitment or roots, it is time for you to act, to go and dig your roots into the "good soil." It is only in Jesus Christ that there is that life.

But be careful, because it is very easy to mistake the rocky ground or the thorns for the good soil. It is not a matter of enthusiasm without commitment, as on the rocky ground. Nor is it a matter of having roots in faith, in order then to continue living for success, fame, and riches, as among thorns. It is a matter of a radical newness of life, setting out new roots into a new soil in order to give new and abundant fruit. It is a matter of commitment. It is a matter of rejecting both the passing enthusiasm of the rocky ground and equally passing successes among the thorns.

If you find yourself on the rocky ground, with a faith abundant in enthusiasm but lacking in depth, the answer is the same: the good soil. If you find yourself among thorns, seeking to be faithful, but at the same time running after those forms of success which society rewards, the answer is once again the same: the good soil.

This moving away from the path, or from the rocky ground, or from among thorns, and to the good soil, is what we have been trying to do throughout these last few weeks with Matthew. We are submitting to a discipline, digging roots into the good soil, making a commitment with Jesus Christ and with his purposes for us, for all of society, and even for all of creation. As we develop those roots, we shall be able to understand those purposes better, so that Jesus will be able to say to us "Blessed are your eyes, for they see, and your ears, for they hear" (verse 16).

For Group Study

Besides leading the group in a discussion of all that has been said above, you may employ the following method:

Divide the group into three subgroups and ask the first to think about what would be the meaning of living "on the path." The group may respond by writing a few paragraphs about such a life or may prefer to present it in a brief drama or sketch. What is important is that this style of life, without roots or commitment, be made clear.

Ask the second group to do likewise with life "on rocky ground," and the third to do it with life "among thorns."

Suggest that all three groups, before preparing their presentation, read and discuss what has been said in this chapter about these three manners of life.

Gather the groups together and allow each to make its presentation.

After the presentations, ask: *What would it mean for the sort of person each of you has described to come to the good soil and dig his or her roots into Jesus Christ?*

WEEK
SEVEN

First Day: Read Matthew 13:24-30, 34-43   7-17-05

See: The parables of Jesus are part of his message about the reign of God. Many of them begin with words such as: "The kingdom of heaven may be compared to. . . ." Out of eight parables in Matthew 13, only two begin otherwise: The Parable of the Sower (13:3-9, 18-23) and that of the trained scribe (13:52), but even the latter is explicitly about the kingdom of heaven.

Among the parables to be studied in this chapter, some deal with the manner in which the children of God's reign are to see the evil around them, and others speak of the great value of that reign, a value so high that everything else pales by comparison.

The parable about the weeds among the wheat is an answer to one of the most ancient questions that humankind has always posed: Why do the wicked prosper? Wouldn't divine justice be better served by destroying them? Should not those who are good destroy the wicked on God's behalf? The parable does not respond in philosophical terms but rather says that God has a plan for bringing about the reign, and that this is like a harvest in which the distinction between the just and the unjust will be made. Meanwhile, the just are not to go out seeking to destroy the unjust, for in so doing they are likely to damage the harvest as well.

Judge: This parable points to a great danger confronting those who have decided for the reign of God. The church must be morally and doctrinally pure, and we then set out to achieve this. The result is a church that, rather than a community of joy and gratitude for the salvation that has been attained and for the promised reign of God, becomes a judge for its members, watching over them as only a totalitarian state can do. That attitude gave rise to the Inquisition and still gives rise to all the small inquisitions that we Christians conduct against each other.

The tragedy is precisely in what the parable warns: In the process of pulling up the weeds, the wheat is also damaged. When the church supported the Inquisition, those who suffered were not only the heretics who were burned at the stake but the entire church. When one of us, or a group within the church, becomes a guardian of somebody else's morality, a great deal of damage may ensue for whomever we condemn. But also the entire church suffers damage, for it loses its character as a community of faith and love. It is not our task to separate the weeds from the wheat. God will do this at the proper time. Our task is to bear fruit, to produce our own wheat.

Act: Have you ever become a strict judge in condemning other people? Write down their names, and consider the possibility that you may have been unjust or too severe. Ask for forgiveness both from God and from them.

Second Day: Read Matthew 13:31-35

See: Today's text has two parts. We shall not deal much with the second (verses 34-35), for it was already mentioned and somewhat discussed yesterday. The first part includes two very short parables: the mustard seed (verses 31-32) and the leaven (verse 33). Note that in this case, when speaking of the mustard seed, Jesus is not speaking of faith but of the reign of God. (It is in Matthew 17:20 that Jesus speaks of "faith the size of a mustard seed.")

The two parables speak of the kingdom of God. What they have in common is mostly the smallness of the thing chosen as an example: Both the mustard seed and the bit of leaven seem to be insignificant. Another point they have in common is that both are hidden. In the second, although the NRSV speaks of mixing the yeast in the flour, what the text actually speaks of is hiding it. In the first, the act itself of planting implies burying, and therefore hiding. Finally, a third point that the two parables have in common is the great impact of what began in hidden smallness: the seed becomes a tree and the yeast leavens the entire mass.

All of this means that the kingdom of heaven does not announce itself with noise and fanfare or with an obvious and overwhelming power. Rather—at least for the time being, until the end does come—it comes in the small and hardly perceptible.

Judge: We live in a time and in a society in which it would seem that bigger is always better. If we are in business, we measure our success by the size of our sales. If we are to buy a car, we see commercials telling us that the bigger one is best. Our great heroes are powerful, famous, and influential people.

Even in the church sometimes we follow the same mind-set. If a church is big, has much money, and a beautiful building, it is a good church. If it is poor and small, we do not admire it so much. We seem to think that the big church or the television "ministry" that reaches millions are closer to God and to God's reign than the small church, or the humble Christian whose ministry consists of visiting ailing neighbors.

But Jesus tells us otherwise: The reign of God is like a mustard seed or a bit of leaven.

Act: Think about small and unnoticed places where you have experienced the presence of God's reign. Remember perhaps an act of charity or sacrifice on someone's behalf. Ask yourself: How can I be a sign of the healing reign of God?

Write down your answer, and ask God to support you in it.

Third Day: Read Matthew 13:44-58   7-24-05

See: Today's passage includes three parables (13:44-50), another saying of Jesus (13:51-52), and a narrative about the return of Jesus to his hometown of Nazareth (13:53-58). Read the entire passage, although we will center our attention on the first two parables: the hidden treasure and the pearl of great value.

These two parables stress the great value of the reign of God. But above all they emphasize the need to choose between that kingdom and anything else that we may consider valuable. In both cases the story is about someone finding something of great value, who then, in order to possess it, goes and sells all. The teaching is clear: Whoever truly finds the reign of heaven is ready to sacrifice everything for it.

Judge: In a way, these two parables confirm what we have seen repeatedly in this study: One has to choose between the values of the coming reign of God and the values of the present reign; between the purposes of God and those of society around us. The merchant who finds the pearl of great value must choose between that pearl and all the rest. The man who finds the treasure underground has to choose between that treasure and everything else he has. There are no "credit" transactions here, so that we can buy the pearl of great value without getting rid of the others. Selling the other pearls means abandoning everything else that may seem valuable but which conflicts with the values of the kingdom. Nothing can be compared in its value with God's reign.

Act: At this point, we have to ask ourselves: What must we leave behind in our quest for God's reign? The point here is not to congratulate ourselves by making a list of those things we have already left behind but rather to survey our present life in order to find what those other things are that we must still abandon.

Ask yourself: What are some of the things I may have to sacrifice for the sake of God's reign? What customs, practices, desires, ambitions, or dreams that I hold are opposed to the reign of God?

Write down these things in your notebook. Pray, asking God to give you the strength to set them aside. After your prayer, if you have really decided to abandon these things, tear the list off of your notebook, shred it into pieces as you affirm your decision, and throw it away. (From now on, the torn page in your notebook will be a reminder of your decision.)

Fourth Day: Read Matthew 14:1-12

See: We now come to a narrative portion in the Gospel of Matthew. If you have a red-letter Bible, you will see the contrast between chapters 10–13, where most is in red letters, and chapter 14, where there are only a few brief words from Jesus. In this section Matthew is telling us about events in the life of Jesus.

Today's passage tells us of the death of John the Baptist. Note that this does not mean that his death took place at this time in the ministry of Jesus. On the contrary, it had taken place much earlier, and Matthew now tells us about it so we may understand why some thought that Jesus was John the Baptist who had been raised from the dead.

The story of the imprisonment and death of John the Baptist is a story of corruption and weakness on Herod's side and of firmness and courage on John's. John was imprisoned because he condemned Herod's crime. And he was killed for the same reason, since Herodias, who took offense at John's preaching, planned his death.

Judge: John the Baptist did not flee from controversy, and he paid for that with his life. Review in your mind the story of the prophets of Israel, asking yourself how many of them fled from controversy. Did Jesus flee from it? Certainly not, as is clear from all that we have read and will be reading in the next few weeks.

And yet, some Christians seem to think that those who are true disciples of the Lord should never be involved in controversies. Their preaching and witness must be such that no one is upset, that they critique no one, and that all can agree. Thus, if a preacher criticizes something that is taking place in the community, there is always someone who says that such controversial matters should have no place in the pulpit.

What do you think about this? Can there be a really important subject that does not cause controversy? If Christians are not to speak about debatable issues, what will they speak about?

Why is it that so often we Christians or the church at large flee from controversy? Could it be that we value our security, comfort, and prestige above truth?

Act: Think of some pressing need in your community, or some injustice, about which few dare speak. Pray for God's guidance and be ready to say whatever has to be said. Jot down your decision and your thoughts on this matter.

Fifth Day: Read Matthew 14:13-21 *7-3l-05*

See: The story is well known, particularly since it has parallels in all four Gospels, and even here in Matthew there is a parallel event in chapter 15. Note that, according to Matthew, these events took place when Jesus heard that John had been killed. Since the work of John took place long before this particular moment in the Gospel narrative, this means that such narrative is not to be taken as a biography in the strict sense, with a fixed chronological order. On the contrary, Matthew orders his materials with a view to presenting Jesus as the promised Messiah. That is why he joins into a single sermon (the Sermon on the Mount) many of the teachings of Jesus that the other Gospels present separately.

In any case, here we are told that Jesus had compassion for the crowd. The same expression was found earlier in Matthew 9:36, and it was on the basis of this compassion that Jesus sent the disciples on their mission. Here, compassion has to do with the hunger that people are suffering, and that is why Jesus tells his disciples to feed the crowd.

Judge: What does the passage tell us today? First, it tells us that Jesus is concerned not only for people's souls but also for their bodies. And if Jesus is concerned, so also must we be. Some people think that Christianity has to do only with the salvation of the soul. But here Jesus shows us that the same compassion that he has for souls he also has for hungry bodies.

Second, it is clear that we do not have power to feed a crowd with a few loaves and fish. However, what is demanded of us is not that we do what we cannot but that we do what we can. The disciples have five loaves and two fish. They have no more. That is what Jesus demands of them. Jesus does not demand miracles. He demands dedication.

Likewise, when we today read this account, rather than becoming frustrated because we do not have the power of Jesus, we are to respond with obedience, turning over to him what we have so that he may use it with his own power and according to his own will. Jesus does not demand miracles from us, just as he did not demand them from his first disciples. He demands dedication—dedication of what we have and dedication of what we are.

Act: If you compare what you have with the need of the world, the disproportion is as great as the disproportion between the hunger of that crowd and the loaves and fish the disciples had. But these resources are all you have. And that is all that the Lord asks of you.

Would you give them to him?

Sixth Day: Read Matthew 14:22-36

See: This story is also well known. Jesus sends his disciples ahead of him to the other side of the Sea of Galilee, and late at night he comes to them walking on the water. Peter comes out to meet him, also walking on the water, but he begins to sink and Jesus holds him up while he says: "You of little faith, why did you doubt?"

The most common interpretation of this story is that Peter's faith faltered when he saw the strong wind, and this is the reason he began to sink. But if we read the passage carefully, we will note that it was Peter who asked Jesus to allow him to walk on the water. Peter says: "Lord, if it is you, command me to come to you on the water" (verse 28). Thus, his initial lack of faith was in doubting that it was indeed Jesus who was coming to him. His attempt to walk on water is a way of testing Jesus. In a way, Peter walks on water not because he has faith but because he doubts. That is why, when the wind becomes strong, faith is insufficient, and Peter begins to sink.

Judge: In our time, it has become quite common to put faith to the test in a manner very similar to Peter's. Some tell us that if we really have faith, all that we ask from God will be given to us. But that faith must be proved by extraordinary events.

A faith that needs to be proved is lack of faith. Peter asks Jesus to allow him to walk on water because he is not certain that it is Jesus that is coming to him on the water. Likewise, whoever has to test the power of faith by constantly asking for more and renewed miracles, is actually lacking in faith. Faith does not demand proof. Faith trusts and waits. Had Peter really trusted that this was the Lord coming to him, he would simply have done what the rest did: wait for Jesus and worship him. But he tried to test Jesus, and the result was that he himself was tested and found wanting.

In reality, the supposed faith that is constantly demanding confirmation is actually testing God. It claims to be faith but only believes when a miracle confirms it; and when there is no miracle, it will not believe. That is what Jesus calls a person "of little faith."

Act: Write the following in your notebook: *Lord I believe. Help my unbelief.* Ask God to give you a firm faith, one that does not need confirmation or proof.

Seventh Day: Read Matthew 15:1-20   8 14-05

See: We now return to the controversy of Jesus with the scribes and Pharisees. We are not told that all the scribes and Pharisees came to Jesus asking these questions. It is important to note that not all the scribes and Pharisees were opponents of Jesus. (See Matthew 13:52.)

At any rate, the scribes and Pharisees pose a question which is a complaint, perhaps even an accusation: "Why do your disciples break the tradition of the elders?" And then they explain that the disciples are breaking that tradition by not washing their hands before eating.

(At this point it is important to understand that this had little to do with hygiene, as when we say today that it is important to wash one's hands before eating. It was rather a matter of ritual purity. There was always the danger that one might have touched something ritually impure or contaminated, and that then, by eating without washing one's hands, one would allow that uncleanness to enter the body.)

Jesus answers with an even stronger accusation. If the disciples break "the tradition of the elders," these scribes and Pharisees break "the commandment of God." Then follows the explanation as to why Jesus accuses them of breaking the commandment of honoring father and mother (verses 4-9). Jesus tells them that they refuse to honor their parents as God commands by claiming that they are bound by offerings and sacrifices. This refers to the manner in which someone not wishing to help another, even though in theory such help was an obligation, could avoid it simply by consecrating to God those resources which should have been employed for helping the needy.

If, for instance, my father was in need of something, and I had the money to give to him but did not wish to do so, all that I would have to do is declare that the money is an offering consecrated to God. As a result, according to Jesus, I would have broken the commandment of God.

Note the contrast between the commandment and the tradition. Jesus does not say that the tradition is evil, but he does accuse the Pharisees and the scribes of making use of tradition in order to avoid obeying the commandment. What they are doing is " 'teaching human precepts as doctrines' " (verse 9).

Then Jesus widens the discussion, bringing the crowd into it. Clearly contradicting what the scribes and Pharisees just said, Jesus declares that "it is not what goes into the mouth that defiles a person, but it is what comes out of the mouth that defiles."

The disciples, who are able to move freely about the crowd and hear the reaction of the Pharisees, come and tell Jesus that the Pharisees are offended by what he has just said.

Rather than trying to mollify the Pharisees, Jesus tells his disciples that whatever God did not plant will be uprooted; that is to say, the teachings of those Pharisees who confuse human traditions with divine commandments will not prevail. He then refers to them as "blind guides of the blind," pointing out that "if one blind person guides another, both will fall into a pit."

When Peter asks for an explanation, Jesus tells him that defilement comes not from without but from within. In the end, all that is eaten goes into the sewer. The reason for this wording is to explain that evil intentions and all other sorts of evil do not enter through the mouth but rather spring from the heart. These are the things that truly defile a person, and not those that the Pharisees declare to be impure and unclean.

Judge: It is easy to speak about the Pharisees and the scribes of time past and how they used their traditions in order to disobey God's will. But if we remain there, we have not really dealt with the passage for ourselves. Once we have understood why the Pharisees broke the commandment, it is important for us to consider the possibility that we might be doing the same.

Throughout history, Christians have been at least as creative as those ancient Pharisees in finding ways to invalidate the will of God, especially by means of human tradition. Examples abound. Reference has already been made to the Inquisition. Part of the tragedy of the Inquisition was that it destroyed many people by accusing them of errors that were sometimes minute. Human traditions, and a particularly narrow way of understanding the Christian faith, were used in order to break the Great Commandment of love.

Likewise, in the time of the Protestant Reformation, and shortly thereafter, there were Christians who insisted that the only proper way to worship God was with the Psalms and who, therefore, rejected every other form of music or hymn. The result was that in rejecting those hymns and that music, they also rejected the Christians who used them. Once again, human tradition was used in order to break the commandment of love.

I know of a church where there is strong insistence that the only legitimate position for prayer is kneeling. Anyone who dares to remain seated or standing during a prayer is accused of not being truly biblical. However, is it not the case that the church itself is antibiblical in that it breaks and ignores the commandment of love?

Think about your church. Are there traditions or customs that, like those of the scribes and Pharisees, run the risk of denying the commandments of God? Let us consider some possibilities:

There are churches that, without declaring it openly and sometimes even without knowing it, place ethnic or racial obstacles along the path of any who wish to be part of them. Sometimes they do not exclude such people openly but simply receive them coldly, do not give them opportunities for service, or exclude them from committees or other centers of decision making so that in the end they leave. This may happen most commonly among white people who "accept" those of other races and cultures, but not fully. However, it happens also in ethnic minority churches, where quite often one subgroup controls everything and receives the other subgroups with less than full enthusiasm. Quite often, churches marginalize people on the basis of social class or level of education.

How is this done? On the basis of human traditions—traditions that in themselves are good but that are then employed to exclude others. The meals that are typical of one group are preferred and served over those of another group. There is insistence on worshiping with the hymns that a particular group knows and appreciates while rejecting the rhythms and traditions of other lands. In the end, the church becomes a sort of social club where a particular cultural tradition is cherished and celebrated while those who do not belong to it are made to feel alien and unwelcome. Thus is the commandment of God—of going and making disciples—invalidated.

Another example: There are churches whose customs seem to be just as sacred as the gospel itself. *The service of worship has to be held at eleven because it has always been held at eleven. If someone cannot attend at eleven, tough luck.*

In still other cases those customs are disguised as morality. *Did you see how Jenny dared come to church in such a dress?* or *Jack says that the doctor ordered him to take medicine that has alcohol and that he is drinking it for his health. Can you believe it?*

However, it is time to move beyond such examples. Think of the customs and traditions in your own church and how they may come to occupy the place of the commandment of God or even to invalidate it.

Now think about your own customs, especially those that we often call habits. We all have habits, for without them it is impossible to organize life. When waking, each of us has his or her own routine, a series of habits that are followed practically without thinking. We also know that there are good and bad habits. But what we sometimes forget is that a good habit can be badly employed and then becomes one of those human customs that deny the commandment of God.

In a way, this is what happened in the case of the scribes. They were used to being the interpreters of Scripture, the ones consulted by others. That in itself is good. It is a good custom. But when Jesus came and challenged some of their interpretations and their practices, their very habit of being respected and admired for their biblical erudition became an obstacle between them and obedience to God.

The same may also happen to us with any habit, no matter how good. Those of us who are used to teaching have to make sure that this does not keep us from learning. Those who are used to preaching, have to make sure that this does not keep us from listening attentively to the word of God. If we, who are used to teaching and preaching, believe that we are and forever will be leaders, we are nothing but "blind guides of the blind."

Act: If while thinking about the life of your church you were faced with some customs or traditions that deny the commandment of God—above all, if they deny the commandment of love—decide to discuss this with other members of your congregation in order to find a solution. If others are following this study and, therefore, are studying this text for today, gather them in order to discuss how the church can respond to the problems you have seen. Make sure you do this with kindness and understanding.

Now think about your own customs and the manner in which they express or deny the law of God. There is no doubt that most of our actions are guided by habit. Seldom during the day do we stop and think about what we are doing and why we are doing it. That is why it is important to develop good habits. Decide to develop habits that express your faith.

As an aid in this direction, make a list of your habits that seem to express your faith and of other habits that are an obstacle against such expression. For instance, habits such as the following may impede your witness: lying; always being late while others are waiting for you; allowing your mind to wander when someone else is speaking, as if the other person were unimportant; seeking always what is best for you. The following habits may help you express and communicate your faith: being mindful of others; smiling and greeting people you meet throughout the day; doing favors for those who need them; telling the truth with integrity and without exaggeration. To these we could add "religious" habits, such as praying, studying the Bible, attending church, or tithing.

Once you have made these two lists, decide to strengthen one and to do everything possible to destroy the other. During the coming days, every few days, return to these lists and try to remember occasions in which you have allowed yourself to be dragged along by your bad habits as well as those other occasions in which your good habits have taken you along a path of love and service.

For Group Study

First of all, make sure that the group understands why the Pharisees opposed Jesus. One way to do this may be to ask two or three members of the class to prepare a brief role-play. Suggest that they imagine that they are Pharisees or scribes commenting about Jesus and the disciples. On that basis, they are to prepare a dialogue of no more than three minutes. (If there is a measure of humor in the dialogue, this may make it more interesting for people to remember.)

Stress the contrast that Jesus makes between the commandment of God and human traditions. (Look especially at verse 6.)

Then move to a discussion about the possibility that we as individuals, as a group, or as a church may have customs that deny the commandment of God. Think specifically in terms of the following two commandments:

The commandment to love one another. Do we have customs or practices that, rather than promoting love, actually result in prejudice and misunderstanding?

The commandment to go and make disciples. Do we have customs or habits that impede our witness? Do we have customs that make it difficult for other people to join our community of faith even though they believe as we do?

W E E K
EIGHT

First Day: Read Matthew 15:21-39   *8-14-05*

See: Today's text may be divided into three sections: verses 21-28, the Canaanite woman; verses 29-31, a summary of many other miracles; verses 32-39, another story of the feeding of a multitude.

Since we have earlier discussed similar passages, today we shall center our attention on the first part of the text, that is, the healing of the daughter of the Canaanite woman. An important dimension of this passage is that Jesus is in Gentile territory, "the district of Tyre and Sidon." It is there that this woman approaches him to intercede for her daughter. In order to underscore that this woman is not a Jew, but a Gentile, Matthew relates a dialogue in which Jesus affirms that his mission is above all to the "lost sheep of the house of Israel."

The Canaanite woman insists. Eventually, Jesus grants her request in what seems to be an announcement of later occurrences in the Gospel of Matthew: that the message and work of Jesus will not be only for Israel but for all humankind.

Judge: Compare this passage with the one we studied two days ago, when Peter went to meet Jesus walking on water. The contrast is clear: To Peter, who not only is a good Jew but also one of his first disciples, Jesus says that he is "of little faith" (14:31). To the woman, who is a Gentile— and even more than a Gentile, a Canaanite, a daughter of a people who for centuries have been Israel's most bitter enemy—Jesus declares: "great is your faith" (15:28).

This is because there is a great difference between the two. Peter tries to walk on water, but he does this in order to make sure that the one who comes to him is Jesus. In other words, Peter doubts Jesus, and that is why he asks for a miracle. In contrast to this, the Canaanite woman does not for a minute doubt that Jesus can do what she requests. On the contrary, from the very beginning she calls him, "Lord, Son of David," and she knows that Jesus can help her. Peter wishes to walk on the sea not because he has faith but because he is lacking in it. The Canaanite woman insists that Jesus must save her daughter because she knows that Jesus can do it.

Here we see once again a subject that appears repeatedly in the Gospels: The good Jew, a disciple from the beginning, has no advantage over this Canaanite woman, a late arrival. Even though a Canaanite, this woman's faith places her on the same level as the most faithful and earliest disciples. In God's reign, those who believe they have an advantage must take care lest they be last.

Act: Do you know someone who seems to be far from God's reign because of sin or because of disbelief? Decide to speak to that person about the gospel. Jesus came to the world for all of us.

Second Day: Read Matthew 16:1-12

See: The debate continues with the Pharisees, to whom the Sadducees are now added. (This is the first occasion on which Matthew presents the Sadducees as enemies of Jesus, although in 3:7 he has quoted some harsh words of John the Baptist against them.) As stated before, once again they demand from Jesus a "sign from heaven," a miracle that would be undeniable proof of his mission.

Jesus tells them that when it suits them, they can indeed discern the signs of the times. All they have to do is look at the sky in order to know if it is going to rain. But when it comes to Jesus and the many "signs" around him, all that they have seen does not suffice. Jesus repeats what he said before: the only sign to be given to them will be "the sign of Jonah."

Shortly thereafter Jesus warns his disciples to guard against "the yeast of the Pharisees and the Sadducees." At first the disciples do not understand, but finally they see that what Jesus means is that they are to guard against "the teaching of the Pharisees and Sadducees."

Judge: This passage reminds us of Peter when he saw Jesus walking on the water and demanded a sign that it was indeed Jesus. The Pharisees and Sadducees were supposed to be good Jews, believers in God. Like Peter, they had already witnessed sign after sign, miracle after miracle; but they still required more. The truth is that they do not wish to believe, and therefore, no sign will be sufficient for them. For those who do not wish to believe, there is no miracle that is powerful enough to force belief, for it is always possible to explain away a miracle. For those who believe, miracles are not necessary.

The Pharisees and Sadducees ask for a sign not because they wish to believe but because by doing so they can postpone their believing. That is "the yeast" of the Pharisees and the Sadducees. Like all yeast, it acts almost imperceptibly, but eventually it affects everything.

Act: Are you one of those who say, *If God would simply show me by means of a miracle or sign what I should do, I certainly would.* In that case, beware of the yeast of the Pharisees and Sadducees! What the Pharisees and Sadducees wish to do is blame God for their own disobedience: It is God who has not given them a clear enough sign.

The truth is that God has given us thousands of signs, and if you and I do not obey, the reason is simply that we do not wish to do so. Go back to what you have written in your notebook in past sessions. Have you done as you promised? Do you believe that with a clear "sign," you would have done it?

Third Day: Read Matthew 16:13-20 8-21-05

See: The text is well known. Jesus asks the disciples about the opinions circulating regarding himself, and they tell him that many think that he is a prophet from the past who has returned, such as John the Baptist or Elijah. These were supposed to have been forerunners of the Messiah. Therefore, apparently people were saying that Jesus himself was a forerunner of the Messiah.

The conversation continues, and Simon Peter finally makes his famous statement: "You are the Messiah, the Son of the living God." In other words, Jesus is not one of those forerunners, but the Messiah himself. (Some versions say, "You are the Christ." The word *Christ* is simply the Greek translation of the Hebrew word *Messiah*, which means *anointed*.)

Immediately Jesus gives Simon a new name, Peter, which means *rock*. Then Jesus relates that new name with the manner in which Peter will be a rock on which Jesus will build his church.

Judge: This passage has been so involved in debates between Catholics and Protestants that it is difficult to read without that background in mind. However, try to read it in a different way, seeking in it a word of God for you.

Note that the passage deals with identity. First, it is the identity of Jesus as discussed among people and which Simon Peter clarifies by declaring that Jesus is the Messiah. Second, Jesus turns to Simon's identity, giving him a new name, Peter. To the "you are" of Simon (verse 16), Jesus responds with another "you are" (verse 18). This is what happens when one confesses Christ. Not only do we confess him but also at that very moment Jesus gives us a new identity, which in this particular case is symbolized by a new name.

That new name does not serve only to remind Simon Peter of this particular moment in his life but also to give him a new purpose and mission: "You are Peter, and on this rock I will build my church."

When Jesus calls us, he does not simply call us to believe in him but also to serve him. When Jesus makes us new creatures, he also gives us a new purpose in life, a new mission.

Act: What is your purpose in life? What is the mission that has been entrusted to you? Think about it. Talk with others who may help you find and clarify this. Write down your thoughts.

Fourth Day: Read Matthew 16:21-28

See: Immediately after Peter's confession, Jesus begins to speak to his disciples, not about the glory that was expected to surround the Messiah but about the sufferings awaiting him in Jerusalem. Peter does not want that to happen. Jesus, who has just praised him and given him a new name, now gives him still another name: Satan. Why? Because "you are setting your mind not on divine things but on human things." There are two ways of looking at things. From the human point of view, the cross is evil and must be avoided. But from God's point of view, it must be claimed. That is true about Jesus and is also true about his followers. From the point of view of human taste, desire, and comfort, the cross—giving up life—is a loss. But from the point of view of God and divine purposes, it is a profit.

Judge: To save one's life is to lose it, and to lose it is to find it. If we do not understand that and do not seek to live according to it, we are like Peter when he was trying to dissuade Jesus. We do not understand the things that are of God, but only human things. In that case, we are a stumbling block. In that case, we may well hear Jesus saying: "Get behind me, Satan! You are a stumbling block to me."

Specifically, what is the meaning of taking up the cross?

Taking the cross is an active action. It is not simply accepting with resignation whatever befalls us but rather choosing that which would normally be even repugnant to us. The cross is not just a sign of suffering. It was above all an instrument of torture, as is the electric chair, the scaffold, or the firing wall. Taking up the cross does not mean only walking through life with a burden but walking toward Calvary. It is a harsh word to say that we have to choose such a thing. However, that is actually what Jesus said. Christian life is not a matter of life or death but a matter of life and death. It is a matter of dying in order to live.

However, this does not mean simply giving up something. Jesus does not ask us to suffer for the pleasure of suffering. (That is a mental illness called masochism.) What Jesus tells us is that we are to be so committed to God's reign and its justice that this will bring about the sufferings that inevitably follow from such commitment. Jesus did not go to Jerusalem because he wanted to suffer, nor because he liked to suffer, but rather because that was what the hour required of him.

Act: The question we must then ask ourselves is *What is it that God's reign and God's justice demand of us?* Think about that. Not asking such a question is trying to save your life and therefore, Jesus tells us, actually losing it. Therefore, ask it, knowing that you will have to accept the crosses and sufferings that will come as a consequence of your answer. Write down your answers and reflections.

Fifth Day: Read Matthew 17:1-13   2-6 -05

See: This passage is usually called "The Transfiguration," because Matthew tells us that "he was transfigured before them," and he allowed them to see something of his glory. Immediately, Moses and Elijah appeared, walking with Jesus. Remember that Moses was the giver of the law, and Elijah was the first of the great prophets. Therefore, the presence of these two is a symbol of the entire law and the prophets, of the history of God's revelation to Israel. And now Jesus, who talks to them, is the culmination of that history and that revelation.

Peter wishes to build dwellings for the three, but two of them disappear and only Jesus remains, over whom a heavenly voice pronounces words that remind us of his baptism.

On descending from the mountain, Jesus tells them not to tell anyone about what they have seen. Then the disciples ask him about the Jewish expectation that Elijah would return in order to announce the Messiah. Jesus leads them to understand that this has been fulfilled in the person of John the Baptist and that now he himself is the fulfillment of the promises about the Messiah.

Judge: Reading this passage immediately after what we studied yesterday in Matthew 16, we see that Peter is still seeking to evade the cross. Yesterday he tried to dissuade Jesus from going to Jerusalem. Now he suggests he ought to stay on the Mount of Transfiguration. If Jesus agrees to stay on the mountain, the road to Jerusalem will be postponed. But Jesus does not agree. It is necessary to go on to Jerusalem and to the cross. Furthermore, when the disciples ask him about Elijah, Jesus makes use of that opportunity to remind them of what he told them about the need to take up the cross (verse 24). What happened to John the Baptist will also happen to Jesus as well as to his disciples.

Act: Having Jesus tell him once was not enough for Peter. Do not be surprised that you also have to be told more than once. Once and again, Jesus will tell you: *Take up your cross each day and follow me.* Once and again you will have to undertake the walk.

Go back to your thoughts and notes from yesterday. Have they been confirmed today with your life and your decisions? Or have you once again postponed your obedience as Peter wanted to do on the mount? Decide to take the steps necessary to do what you promised yesterday. Pray over it. Discuss it with other people in your faith community. Write down your conclusions, discoveries, and decisions so as not to forget them.

Sixth Day: Read Matthew 17:14-27

See: The passage can be divided into three parts. The first (verses 14-20) is another healing miracle. In the second (verses 22-23), Jesus once again announces his death. The third (verses 24-27) deals with a new theme, and therefore, we shall center our attention on it.

It was a custom for every Jewish male to pay two drachmas for the upkeep of the Temple in Jerusalem. This was not obligatory, for Jewish authorities did not have the power to collect it from those who did not wish to pay, especially if they lived far away. On returning to Capernaum, where Jesus normally attended synagogue, it was natural that he be asked whether he intended to pay the two drachmas or not. The question, rather than about money, was about religious authority. Would Jesus accept and submit to the Temple authorities?

The answer that Jesus gives is that, just as the children of the king do not pay royal taxes, he has no obligation to pay the Temple tax. However, in order not to give offense, he gives them instructions that make it clear that it is actually God who is paying both for him and for Peter.

Judge: Jesus tells Peter that he has no obligation to pay the Temple tax, but even so, in order not to offend people around him, he will submit.

Something similar is true of Christians when it comes to civil law. We are citizens of a higher reign and even children and heirs of a king. This means that human laws and social custom have only a secondary value, but it does not mean that we should disobey them. Just as Jesus obeyed the law of the Temple tax, so also are we to obey the laws and customs of the present reign and society even though we are subjects and heirs of the coming reign of God.

However, just as Jesus had to critique what was done at the Temple and oppose its laws, so must Christians know that all laws passed by the state are secondary as compared with the divine purpose. We are not to disobey them, but we cannot let them force us to disobey God's will.

Are there laws and customs in our society that are opposed to God's will? In that case, what should be our attitude?

Act: Pray in thanksgiving for the state and its laws. Thank God for society and for its customs. Ask God to give you the wisdom and courage to follow those laws and customs, even while knowing that they are secondary to the will of God. Ask also for wisdom and courage to oppose and confront such laws and customs when necessary.

Seventh Day: Read Matthew 18:1-9

See: The passage we are studying presents a progression: First, the disciples pose a question to Jesus. He then answers by taking a child as an example. From that, he moves on to the importance of dealing with the small ones with special care. This then leads him to speak about those who are a stumbling block for others, and finally to speak about the need to be ready to sacrifice whatever may be a hindrance for entering God's reign.

The most common interpretation of this passage is that Jesus is telling us that we must be as innocent as children in order to enter the kingdom of heaven. But when we study the passage carefully we see that this is not really what is being discussed here. The disciples ask Jesus who would be the greatest in God's reign. Naturally, they have an image of a reign of God that looks very much like human kingdoms, where the king has his ministers and high officials, who in turn lord it over the rest and enjoy all sorts of privileges. But Jesus answers by taking a small child, placing it in the center, and declaring that in order to enter God's reign what one has to do is to be humble "like this child." What is important about the child—what the disciples are invited to imitate—is not innocence but humility.

In order to understand this, we must remember that at that time children were seen differently than they are today. Today, children have privileges and protection, and people believe that the greatest treasure of a household is its children. At that time, children received little attention. They were considered unimportant until they grew up. They had practically no rights and were rarely respected. In placing a child "among them," at the center, Jesus is showing them that this one who was marginalized—at the edge of things, as someone who did not count—is now at the center. And he is there not because he has done something, not even because he is innocent, but rather because God is particularly mindful of the small and marginalized.

What the disciples have to do is to become humble like this child. Without that, they will not enter God's kingdom. On the other hand, by doing so they will become "greatest." (Which in turn means that everyone who enters God's reign is already "great.")

But the lesson that Jesus gives them also has other consequences: Anyone who receives one of these small and unimportant ones will be receiving Jesus. And the opposite is also true: There will be terrible punishment for anyone who becomes a stumbling block for "one of these little ones who believe in me."

Jesus then speaks harsh words about how we are to be rid of anything that may become a stumbling block, including a hand, a foot, or an eye.

Judge: Look around you and try to discern who are the "least" in our society and in our community. Sometimes, even today, they are the children because despite all we say about the value of children and their rights to be loved, cared for, nourished, and instructed, there are still many out there who are lacking all of that. There are children who are abused by their families, physically as well as mentally and even sexually. There are children whose parents love them, but do not have the resources to feed them properly. Others attend schools in which the lack of resources and the level of violence are such that they can learn very little. Therefore, children are still among the "least" in our society, and as Christians we have a particular responsibility to them.

Remember also that there are other people in our society who are considered "least," not because they are young or for any such reason but simply because they are undervalued by society just as earlier children were undervalued. And at the lower echelons of the social and economic scale, there are people who are chronically unemployed, whom society considers as disposable. Instead of being considered fellow human beings, they are seen as problems.

This is clear in the manner in which newspapers and politicians speak of such people. For instance, when speaking about the "problem" of the homeless, they are not really referring to the problems such people face but to the homeless themselves as a problem to society. What seems to worry such politicians is not the suffering of the homeless but the manner in which they seem to threaten or at least to besmirch the rest of society.

What shape should humility take when we face such people? Certainly it does not mean abandoning our home and going to sleep on a bench in the park, as one who does not have a room or a roof, although such a night, spent outdoors and with no security, would really help us to understand the plight of these "least." But it certainly does mean at least two things:

First, it means that we have to acknowledge that whatever we have is not due to our being in any way better than those who are in need. Whoever sees a hungry person and rejoices that they themselves are not hungry because they know how to earn bread, while the other person either does not know how or cannot do so, does not deserve to be called a Christian. However, such an attitude is at the very foundation of what many current politicians—and even some who call themselves born-again Christians—tell us about the poor and what we are to do regarding poverty.

Second, to become humble as one of these "least" means to welcome them, to share with them what we have. This can be done at several levels. We may give money and other goods to be used for those in need. (For instance, many churches are involved in programs against hunger, and as Christians, we should all support those programs.) We can also do it through our work, making efforts so that the company that employs us will also hire some who would otherwise be unemployed, or that the same company may make a contribution to the welfare programs already in existence—for instance, those that build homes for the poor. We can also do it at the level of politics, voting for people who are committed to using the resources of the state in the best way possible so that those in greater need will receive most help. And we can do it at the personal and direct level, personally approaching somebody in need in order to see how we can be of help.

Act: Those in need who have just been mentioned—and several others that could be listed—are many: children, the poor, the hungry, the homeless, the abused, the unemployed, and so on. All of these causes deserve our support, and it is crucial that, as a believer in Jesus Christ, you be concerned about them.

There is also an old Spanish saying to the effect that one who attempts to grasp too much cannot grasp very strongly. This points to the danger that being concerned for everyone in need and for all sorts of need, we end up doing nothing for anyone.

Therefore, it is important for today's Bible study to lead you to a commitment to at least a person or a specific cause. Think of all that have been mentioned or of any that have not been mentioned here. Evaluate the resources that you have available to respond to each possible cause or need, such as money, time, gifts, and interest. On the basis of all that, make a commitment to yourself and to God that you will work actively for that cause or that person. After reflection and prayer, write down your commitment.

However, such commitments are stronger and longer lasting if they are not made individually, but with others who will provide a support system for us. Invite others in your church or in your faith community to join you in this commitment.

For Group Study

After studying and discussing the foregoing, discuss the following with the group:

Many of our churches have begun showing a deep concern for the needs of their surrounding community. Were there any such concerns in the earlier history of our congregation? Have they changed, or are they still there? Are there now new needs that should be met?

The very fact that you are following this study shows that you have more education and more ability to read and to study than some of your neighbors. Do we act in such a way that those who have less education are made to feel uncomfortable in our church and tacitly told to go elsewhere? Is there some way that you can use your gifts in order to help them?

W E E K
NINE

First Day: Read Matthew 18:10-14

See: Verse 10 has been the basis on which some have built a theory of guardian angels. The notion that there are special angels for nations, churches, or individuals was common in the Judaism of the time (see Daniel 10:13, Acts 12:15, and Revelation 1:20). At any rate, what is emphasized here is not that these "little ones" have an angel that guides each of their steps but rather that through such angels they have direct access to God. If we think that they are unimportant because they appear dirty, dressed in rags, or sunk in vice, let us not forget that their "angels" are in the very presence of God. Therefore, what is important on the basis of this text is not to develop a theory about angels but rather to act toward the "little ones" with the respect they deserve.

The text does not tell us exactly who "these little ones" are for whom Jesus is concerned. However, in reading the entire passage it becomes clear that they are those for whom no one is concerned, who are seemingly lost and forgotten. That is the meaning of the example of the hundred sheep, one of which is lost. The shepherd is particularly concerned about it, not because it is different but simply because it needs special attention. Once it is found, the shepherd's joy over it is greater than for the other ninety-nine.

Judge: Yesterday we studied about the small ones whom society despises but for whom God shows special interest. Do you see some of the same emphases in the reference to angels in verse 10?

When the shepherd goes seeking the lost sheep, are there perhaps times when the other ninety-nine resent the interest of the shepherd in the lost one? Have you ever seen that in your community of faith? Have you ever felt it?

Act: Go back to your decisions of yesterday. Have you done as you intended? What obstacles have you found on your path? Pray for the strength to continue along the same path. Write down your reflections.

Second Day: Read Matthew 18:15-22

See: Some English translations begin this section with "Therefore." This is an attempt to show a connection which is clearly established in the Greek, but which is very easily lost in translation. What Jesus has just said about "these little ones" is to be applied also within the community of faith. Just as in previous verses, the "little ones" were the lost, here the "little one" is whoever offends a brother or sister. Our natural tendency would be to think that if someone is offended we should be concerned above all for that person. The text points us in the opposite direction.

Within the church, when someone sins against another, the sinner is a lost sheep. The other ninety-nine, including the one who is offended, are still on the path. But that other sheep is at risk of being lost. Within that context, note that verse 15 refers precisely to the possibility that this lost sheep may be found.

Verse 18 shows how important the church is, for this clearly implies that whoever is properly and justifiably severed from the church will also be severed from God's reign.

Finally, verses 21-22 tell us that seeking and restoring lost sheep must be done as many times as necessary. It does not suffice to say, *we forgave, and he sinned again,* but rather we are to continue seeking the lost sheep through constant love and a pardon to be repeated "seventy-seven times"—or, as it is written in other versions, "seventy times seven."

Judge: Unfortunately, too often Christians spend more time fighting among themselves than announcing God's reign. The guidance offered here would be of great help. But there is always the danger that we may use it not to obtain reconciliation or to bring back the lost sheep but rather to win the argument. In such a case, it is important to remember that according to the text studied last week, it is possible to win, not only an argument but even the entire world, and still lose one's soul. Whoever sins against us, if his or her sin is really against us, requires special attention. Whoever does not provide such attention, love, and care but rather tries to crush the other, sins. In that case, we may well be facing one more instance of what the Lord said about the speck in our neighbor's eye and the log in ours.

Act: Is there anyone in your faith community with whom you had a bad experience and are still unable to be reconciled? Look at that person with the same love with which a shepherd looks at his sheep and try to reconcile with that person.

Third Day: Read Matthew 18:23-35

See: In order to understand this story, it may help to realize how much money the servant owed the king—in other words, how much was ten thousand talents. A talent was approximately what a laborer would make in fifteen years. Therefore, what this servant owed would be the equivalent of one hundred and fifty thousand years of labor. It was more than all the taxes collected in ten years in the entire kingdom of Judea. The amount was so high that, for those who heard the parable, it would clearly be a fantastic number, much as if we today were to say "umpteen trillion dollars." In verse 26, when the servant promises to pay everything to the king, those who were listening as Jesus told the parable knew that such a promise could never be fulfilled.

In contrast, this servant later refuses to forgive what is a debt of a hundred denarii. A denarius was the salary of a laborer for one day. Therefore, the entire debt is a bit less than four months of labor. Such an amount would certainly sound realistic to Jesus' early listeners.

In verse 29, the promise of the second servant would obviously be much more genuine than the promise which the first servant had made to the king.

Having seen all this, the king's reaction appears both sensible and fair. Since the servant refuses to forgive such a small amount, he has lost any claim to the enormous forgiveness he had received before, and he will have to pay everything that otherwise would have been forgiven.

Judge: The story may seem strange, until we remember that even today there are people who have stolen hundreds of millions of dollars and go unpunished. In some countries, the very same people go into politics, promising to end crime by dealing harshly with thieves. Naturally, in such cases they are not referring to themselves as thieves but rather to those others who steal a few dollars because they are hungry or needy.

When we encounter such cases, we feel that a profound injustice is being committed.

But, do we ever commit a similar injustice? When I think about all that God has forgiven me, I cannot but confess that this is an unpayable debt, similar to that of the king's servant. However, sometimes I find it difficult to forgive people who owe me much less. Even in church, where we should all have the experience of God's forgiveness in constant memory, sometimes we refuse to forgive each other.

What does the parable mean in such cases?

Act: Did you carry through with your decision to reconcile with someone who offended you? If not, why? No matter what the case may be, decide to forgive such people. Make a strong effort so that your church may be a forgiving community.

Fourth Day: Read Matthew 19:1-15

See: Today's text may be divided in two parts. The first (verses 1-12) deals with divorce. The second (verses 13-15) returns to the subject of children. In studying the matter of divorce and what Jesus says about it, it is important to understand that what is under discussion is not only a matter of sexual or conjugal ethics but also of justice. The practice of divorce in ancient times manifested the worst in a society in which women had no rights. Note that in this passage there is no mention of the possibility that a woman might divorce her husband.

In such a society, that decision was entirely in the hands of the husband, who could divorce his wife whenever and for whatever reason he wished without having to render an account to anyone or to share with her any property or income. Furthermore, if there were children, all parental rights would go to the father, and the woman who had been divorced lost all rights in connection with them. While the Pharisees simply hold themselves to obeying the law, Jesus goes beyond that and raises issues that deal not only with divorce but above all with the condition of the woman who has been divorced by her husband.

This is the link with the second part of the text, about children. As we saw before, children, like women, were undervalued and marginalized. What Jesus does is to place both of them at the center.

Judge: Although we may think that we have advanced much since the first century, in many ways the situation of women and children is still deplorable. Both physical and mental abuse within families is much more frequent than we would like to think. In society at large, women still lack many of the opportunities and options open to men. Simply think about news in recent days, and you will see ample evidence of that.

Think about your own family. Do the males (husband, sons, and others) have the same rights and responsibilities as the females (wife, daughters, and others)? If there are differences, what is the reason for them? Do you believe that they are just? Pose the same questions about your workplace, your school, and so on. Finally, pose them about your own local church.

Act: If you are a woman, decide what immediate steps you are to take in order to gain greater justice both for yourself and for other women. If you are a man, decide what steps you will take to support women in their struggle for justice and recognition.

Fifth Day: Read Matthew 19:16-30

See: After reading the story of the rich young man read the final verse again: "But many who are first will be last, and the last will be first" (verse 30). In tomorrow's passage, and in many others we shall be studying, we will see the same words or others like them. In a way, this is the continuation of a theme that has appeared already throughout the Gospel of Matthew: Those who were at the margins are placed at the center; sinners understand the message better than the religious people; the lost sheep receives more attention than the other ninety-nine.

In this particular case, it is a rich young man who approaches Jesus. Since keeping the law in all its details was not easy for the poor, many thought that the poor were worse sinners than the rich. This young man can at least say that he has kept all the commandments since his youth. Therefore, it was to be expected that he would be ahead of others in that which had to do with God's reign.

However, as a result of the conversation the young man leaves saddened, and Jesus comments how difficult it is for a rich person to enter God's reign. This is one more case in which those who seemed to be first end up being last, and those who thought they were at the center of things are really at the edge.

Judge: Jesus says that it is very difficult for a rich person to enter the kingdom. It is so difficult that it would actually be impossible, apart from a miracle from God, for whom all things are possible (verse 26). However, there are those today who claim that being rich is a sign that one has been faithful. Can both things be true? If not, which is true? What do you think?

Why do you think that after his interview with the rich young man Jesus says many who are first will actually be last, and many last will be first? In the context of his own society, was this young man one of the "first," or one of the "last"? Are there today those whom society, or even the church, consider "first" when in truth they are "last"?

Act: Return to the list that you wrote a few days ago about the "least" whom society undervalues. Is it possible that some of these are called to be "first" in God's reign? Make a decision to approach such people with love, as Jesus himself would. If in the eyes of society you are one of the "first," and go ahead of such people, pray for the strength to place them first.

Sixth Day: Read Matthew 20:1-16

See: Once again, today's text begins with Jesus affirming that "the last will be first, and the first will be last." But this time Jesus clarifies his meaning with a parable.

The parable is simple, although surprising. If you read it keeping in mind today's labor laws, you will see why it is surprising. Apparently the parable is unfair. Some laborers work the entire day and others only one hour. However, all receive the same pay. From the point of view of labor law and custom a great injustice has been committed, and that is precisely the reason those who began working earlier protest.

But in truth a greater justice has been served. Those who began working later did so because no one hired them. Those who began working earlier did this not because they were particularly diligent but because they were fortunate enough to be hired earlier. Therefore, the owner of the vineyard, in paying them all the same wage, manifests a sense of justice greater than those who complain because they worked more and were paid the same. It is a sort of justice based on love and grace. The owner of the vineyard, precisely because he is the owner, has the freedom to pay the last the same as the first.

As was expected, it was the first to arrive who are also the first to protest. After all, they have spent the entire day working. Those who arrived later do not complain but simply accept what is graciously given to them. The result is that the last to arrive, those who know that they have received by grace, are able to accept this strange justice of the owner in a way that is very difficult for those who arrived earlier and worked the entire day. That is why Jesus says that the last will be first and the first will be last.

Judge: Place yourself in the position of those who heard Jesus tell this parable. They were Jews, and therefore people who throughout their lives had sought to serve God. Some were the disciples themselves who had left behind their nets and their other businesses to follow him. Now Jesus tells them that the last will be first, that is, that those who expect to be first because they are Jewish or because they are among his disciples must take care lest they end up being last because they do not know how to receive graciously what God offers out of mere grace.

Think about yourself and your faith community. Is there the danger that we think because we are Christians, because we attend church, or because we study the Bible, that we are necessarily ahead of those who do not do so? Above all, is there the danger that when such people come to faith we will deal with them as recent arrivals, as people who have fewer rights than we do. When we do that, are we not placing ourselves "first," and therefore condemning ourselves to be "last"?

Act: Remember that, from the point of view of the long history of God's action in humankind, you and I are latecomers, laborers of the last hour.

Pray for the following: that God help you to remember that all that you are and all that you have, you have received by God's grace and not by your own merit; and that God help you to place first those whom society and even the church deem to be last.

Seventh Day: Read Matthew 20:17-28

See: The text begins by repeating what Jesus has already said to his disciples: that he goes to Jerusalem to suffer, die, and finally rise again.

But what then follows is very different. The mother of two of the disciples approaches Jesus and, completely ignoring the terrible and painful things he has said, asks him for special privileges for her sons in the kingdom of God. The two disciples want to sit in special places, one at the right hand of the Lord and one at his left, which also implies special power and authority. Thus, while they certainly show that they trust the coming of God's reign, they also show almost incredible insensitivity, asking for favors precisely at the moment when Jesus has just been speaking of his crucifixion.

Jesus invites them to drink of his cup. (Some manuscripts also add sharing in his baptism.) In other words, he invites them to share his own lot, which he has just said is one of suffering and crucifixion. When they, too, accept that lot Jesus tells them that they will indeed be part of it but that even this will not give them special places in God's reign.

All of this brings quarrels among the disciples. Then Jesus tells them that they still have not understood the strange order of God's reign. Among the nations, rulers lord it over others, and those who are great use their authority. But in God's reign things are very different (see verses 26-27). Beware of seeking to gain a position in God's reign in the same manner in which one gains a position in human kingdoms! Finally, he relates all of this to himself. The reason Christians are not to try to lord it over each other, as takes place among the Gentiles, is that Jesus himself "came not to be served but to serve, and to give his life a ransom for many" (verse 28).

In other words, the different attitude that Christians should have is grounded in the person of Jesus Christ himself. The reason the order of God's reign is to be different is that the lordship of Jesus is also different. Jesus did not come to be served, but to serve. Once again, the life, passion, death, and resurrection of Jesus are the pattern by which all Christian life is to be measured. At this point what Jesus has said about taking up the cross gains a new dimension: We must find a way to be of service.

Judge: Throughout these weeks we have repeatedly seen the contrast between the order of God's reign and the order of human society. We have noted such contrast at various points. At the beginning of these studies, we discussed how our Christmas celebrations may be such as to give clear witness of the One who was born in Bethlehem and of his reign. Later on we saw that the parables spoke of God's reign and also that the miracles of Jesus are an announcement of it.

Now, we finally reach the heart of the contrast between the order of God's reign and the present order. What determines a social order is the manner in which power and resources are distributed. In a monarchy, power belongs to the ruler, who has the authority to distribute positions and resources according to his will. In a plutocracy, power belongs to the rich, who then use it to keep the sort of social order that is most convenient to them. In an industrial corporation, power belongs to the chief executive officer, who uses it to tell each person what to do.

In all of these cases, power usually begets more power. But in God's reign things are very different. The manner in which one attains power is by serving. Strange though it may seem, those who seek power over the rest will end up serving. For us, this should have a clear and direct application. We live in a society where one of the main goals of many people is to have power and authority over others. The more we command, the more important we think we are.

The same is unfortunately true in the church. A member of a class wants to be its president. The pastor of a particular church wants to be the pastor of a larger or more prestigious one. Another wishes to be a superintendent or bishop. In a thousand subtle ways we take it for granted that the higher the post, the better Christians we are.

The church certainly needs managers and people with authority, but that authority is given to them so that they may serve others. When it becomes the authority to use power in such a way that we consider ourselves to be superior, it loses its very reason to exist, which is serving. Within the church, the only truly valid authority is that which serves the last and the least.

Act: Decide that during the next twenty-four hours you will serve someone who, from a merely human point of view, has no right to be served by you. You do not have to decide now what it is that you will do, nor does it have to be something spectacular. Simply make certain that you find a way to render a favor to someone who cannot repay you, who does not deserve it, and perhaps even will not be grateful for it. Tomorrow write down in your notebook the results of your resolve. Try to turn this into a daily practice.

For Group Study

After studying the passage itself, discuss with the group the subject of greatness in the kingdom of heaven. To that end, you may tell the group about a story: when Alexander the Great met the great philosopher Diogenes, who called himself "a dog." Alexander, the great conqueror, visits Diogenes, who lives in a barrel. Alexander offers him anything he wants, and the philosopher simply answers that all he wants is for

Alexander to move aside so that the sun will still shine in his barrel. The king boasts of his power, and the philosopher of his independence. When Alexander declares that he has the best of food, Diogenes responds that plain bread is enough for him; and when the king boasts of his good wine and golden goblets, Diogenes brags of the water he drinks in his hand.

From the point of view of the gospel, is either of the two right? Certainly, Alexander's understanding of his greatness leaves much to be desired, and we will all agree that this is very different from what is called "greatness" in God's reign. But let us not be too quick to condemn Alexander, for many of us, if we could, would live like him, and many of us have made his regal lifestyle the goal of our lives.

What can we say then about Diogenes? Is his actually the "greatness" of God's reign? There certainly is something admirable about a man who is able to live as simply as Diogenes. But, ultimately, even this sort of simple life does not lead to greatness according to Jesus. True greatness is only to be found in serving others.

W E E K

TEN

First Day: Read Matthew 20:29-34

See: At first glance, this is simply one more of the many stories in which Jesus heals the sick. That certainly is the subject here, but there are also other dimensions to the story that stand out as we take into account the context of the narrative.

Jesus is approaching Jerusalem. The reason he will find opposition and death there is that there are powerful people who cannot accept him as the Messiah.

First of all, there are the Romans, who are the ultimate rulers of the land and, therefore, cannot tolerate the notion that someone may claim to be God's anointed, who is expected to restore Israel and the throne of David.

Second, there are the Jewish leaders, political as well as religious, who serve Roman power. They like things just as they are, and the last thing they want is for someone to come up saying he is about to restore the throne of David.

Third, there is the vast majority of the population of Jerusalem, who feel no great enthusiasm for Romans nor for the religious and political leaders who serve the foreign powers. But they know if there is a rebellion, or if someone claims to be the Messiah and manages to get a strong following, the Romans will intervene militarily, and the measure of autonomy that Israel now enjoys will disappear.

When Jesus and his disciples leave Jericho on the way to Jerusalem, there are two blind men who shout: "Lord, have mercy on us, Son of David!" In so doing they are proclaiming Jesus to be the Messiah. Perhaps that is the reason the crowd orders them to be quiet. What they are shouting is subversive and even dangerous. It is dangerous for Jesus himself, who will eventually be crucified on the accusation of having claimed to be "the king of the Jews." It may even be dangerous for the crowd if they simply stand by. But Jesus, rather than ordering the blind men to be silent in order to protect his own interests and avoid difficulties, listens to them, asks them what they want, and grants it to them.

Judge: We live in a time in which people are very much concerned over their image. Even the church is concerned over its image, over how society will see it. We want people to speak well of the church and to do so in such a way that it does not create problems for us. Perhaps we are afraid that if people begin speaking of the church as a strong defender of the poor, this will create problems with the rich and perhaps even hurt income.

We do the same as individuals. We do not wish people to speak ill of us. Nor do we want them to speak well of us for reasons that may be controversial.

In so doing we do not follow the example of Jesus, who listened to the blind men who were shouting dangerous words. Rather than being concerned over his own security, he responded to their need.

Were we to follow the example of Jesus, what would people say of us?

Act: Think of the image that you are trying to project. Write down as many traits of that image as you can, such as joy, hard work, wisdom, responsibility, and so forth. Now think about which of these things makes you a better Christian and which do not. Scratch over those that are not helpful, and pray that God will help you become a better Christian.

Second Day: Read Matthew 21:1-11   3-20-05

See: We are finally at Jerusalem. Note that we are barely entering chapter 21. This final week of the life of Jesus from the entry into Jerusalem to Easter will take seven chapters, a fourth of the entire Gospel of Matthew.

It is common to contrast the attitude of the crowd at the triumphant entry into Jerusalem with the attitude of the same crowd at the trial of Jesus. The text, however, does not say that they are the same people. Perhaps it will be better to understand the narrative as follows: Jesus is on his way to Jerusalem, and he is joined by many people who eagerly await the Messiah. These are the ones who spread their cloaks on the road and cut branches from the trees, and then shout: "Hosanna to the Son of David!" But this is not all the population of Jerusalem. On the contrary, verse 10 tells us that the people in Jerusalem did not know who it was whose entry into Jerusalem was causing such a stir. Later on in the narrative, it will be the inhabitants of Jerusalem itself who will shout: "Crucify him!" They are more traditional Jews than those from Galilee and other areas, and many of them are connected with the existing order.

Judge: When reading the entire story of the passion, do not forget the conflicts between Galileans and Judeans. Today we use the term *Jew* to refer to anyone of that faith, and clearly in that sense, Jesus, Peter, and all the others around them were Jews. But in ancient times the same term would be used usually to refer to those who lived in Judea. Therefore, while Jesus and his disciples are Jewish in the religious sense, they are not Judeans, that is, they are not from Judea itself. Actually, Judeans looked down on Galileans. Taking that into account, you will see that much of what is happening in the story of the passion has to do with the resistance of Judeans to this upstart from Galilee and to his disciples, who are also Galileans.

Do you know similar situations in which foreigners, or people who are in any way different from the majority of the residents of a place, are treated as second-class people?

Have you yourself experienced the pain and confusion that this produces?

Keep these experiences in mind as you read the story of the passion of Jesus.

Act: Think of whatever experience best helps you to understand what it means to be a minority that somehow seems to threaten the traditional privileges of the majority. This may be on the basis of race, culture, or any of the many excuses that people use to discriminate among themselves. Now read the story of the passion and especially of the trial of Jesus. What do you think people in Jerusalem had in mind when they said, "This is the prophet Jesus from Nazareth in Galilee"? What would a Judean think? What would a Galilean think? Write down your reflections.

Third Day: Read Matthew 21:12-22

See: Today's passage includes two apparently disconnected episodes: the cleansing of the Temple and the cursing of the fig tree. However, as we study them we shall see that they are indeed related.

In the first story (verses 12-16) Jesus throws out of the Temple those who were comfortably and profitably placed in it. Changing money and selling doves for sacrifices were necessary services because pagan coins, with their symbols of pagan gods, were not acceptable as offerings. Doves and other animals for sacrifice had to be perfect and declared acceptable by the priests. Therefore, Jesus is not complaining that such activities are taking place but rather that they are being used to strengthen the powerful and increase the prestige of the priests, while those who do not have enough to buy and sell are left out.

That is why, immediately after Jesus casts out those who were expected to have a position of privilege within the Temple, Matthew tells us that the blind and the lame came to him, and he healed them. Immediately after that, the priests and the scribes become angry because "the children" are praising Jesus. In response, Jesus tells them that "infants and nursing babies" will speak the praise of God.

On that basis, the episode about the fig tree becomes one of those acted-out preachments that were common among the prophets of Israel. By drying up the fig tree because it produces no fruit, Jesus offers a dramatic example of what he has repeatedly affirmed: those who bear no fruit will be cut down.

Judge: It is not often that we hear sermons about the cursing of the fig tree. Why do you think that is the case? Could it be because here we see that Jesus is not only the loving and forgiving friend but also the judge who demands fruit? Could it be because this story shows us the severe face of God, who has placed us so that we may bear fruit and who will demand fruit from us? If that is the case, what sort of fruit should you be bearing?

How would you explain this passage to a ten-year-old child who knows and sings, "Jesus loves me," but who would have difficulty understanding a Jesus who causes a tree to wither?

Act: Think about the following: If Jesus were to come to you today asking for fruit, what would you answer?

Then, imagine that you are at the end of your days. You are in the presence of the Lord, and an angel is reading a list of your "fruits."

What would you wish the angel to read?

Write it down. Make this a goal for your life.

Fourth Day: Read Matthew 21:23-46

See: Today's story deals with the conflict between Jesus and "the chief priests and the elders of the people." These are the religious elite of Israel, the most venerable and respected, the guardians of religion. They are the ones who hold religious authority over the nation. Now they ask Jesus by what authority he is acting.

Jesus answers with a question and two parables. The question has to do with the authority of John the Baptist. The ones who questioned him now find themselves facing a dilemma. They cannot say that John's authority came from God, for they refused to follow him. Nor can they deny that authority, for John is popular and respected. In other words, Jesus is reminding them that they rejected John, and they are now trying to forget it.

The first parable contrasts the son who says he will obey but does not, with the one who says that he will not obey but finally is obedient. The point should be clear: These chiefs of Israel are like the son who declared himself to be very obedient but was not. In contrast to this, the tax collectors and the prostitutes, without religious fanfare, are going into the kingdom of God ahead of the religious leaders.

The second parable says that those who were left in charge of the vineyard but were not faithful to its owner, will be set aside and destroyed. Once again, the point should be clear: These chiefs of Israel, guardians of God's vineyard, have not fulfilled their responsibility and will be dispossessed.

Judge: It is easy to apply these sayings and parables of Jesus to the chiefs of Israel, and then to remain quite content, because this has nothing to do with us. Indeed, the church has done precisely that quite often, and the result has been that it has felt quite satisfied, declaring that the Jews were disobedient, and therefore, the church (that is, us) has taken their place. But things are not that simple.

First of all, note that "the people" (that is, the rest of Israel) did support Jesus (verse 46). Second, the purpose of God's word is not to lead us to think about the disobedience of past peoples and generations but rather to call us to obedience. Is it perhaps true that at least on some occasions we are like the son who pretended to be obedient but was not, or like the wicked tenants, who acted as if the vineyard were theirs and tried to ignore the owner? There is no doubt that, one way or another, we have all promised an obedience that we have not fulfilled, and we have all failed in the responsibilities entrusted to us by God. In such a case, the only path open to us is repentance and renewed obedience.

Act: Leaf back through your notebook until you find something that you promised but did not do. Repent before God, reaffirm your promise, and ask for strength and direction to fulfill it.

Fifth Day: Read Matthew 22:1-14

See: Today's passage is in a way a double parable, for when we think that it is finished and that we know its teaching, it continues and leads to a further point.

Up to verse 10, the parable is very similar to the two we studied yesterday. A king prepares a great wedding feast for his son, and when those he has invited refuse to attend (and some even rebel, killing the king's emissaries), the king orders people to be invited who normally would not attend such a feast. His emissaries are to go "into the main streets," inviting any they meet. Thus, while the original invitees were left out, there will be other unexpected guests, even people apparently unworthy of such an honor.

Up to this point, the parable seems to confirm what was said by the two earlier parables—the one about the two sons and the one about the wicked laborers in a vineyard. If the original guests think that their initial invitation suffices for them to lead into God's reign, they are sadly mistaken. If the initial invitees do not obey, the king will simply invite others.

But the parable continues. One could almost say that what follows is a different parable. The king goes to see the guests and finds someone who is not appropriately dressed. This is an insult to royal majesty and to the importance of the event. Therefore, the king orders the person to be bound and thrown out.

Judge: Several of the parables studied to this point tell us that those who believe they are close to God's reign simply because they are religious leaders, because they belong to Israel or in our case, because we belong to the church, must take care lest they be left outside. This is reinforced by the first part of the parable. Once again, the last are first, and those on the margin are brought into the center.

However, those who are on the margin cannot count on entering God's reign simply because they are "last." Jesus says that tax collectors and prostitutes "go ahead" of the scribes and Pharisees into God's reign; but this certainly does not mean all prostitutes, by the mere fact of being such, "go ahead." They go ahead only if they repent. But if they count on the king sending invitations widely and do not make the necessary preparations, they too will be left out of the great feast.

In other words, just as it does not suffice to be among the first invitees, it also does not suffice to be among the last. It is necessary to respond to the invitation. It is necessary to be dressed for the feast. It is necessary to be obedient.

Act: Read the following poem, "To-morrow," by Lope de Vega, translated by Henry Wadsworth Longfellow, thinking about your own experience and in an attitude of prayer (if you need to do so, read it more than once until you understand its import):

> LORD, what am I, that, with unceasing care,
> Thou didst seek after me, that thou didst wait,
> Wet with unhealthy dews, before my gate,
> And pass the gloomy nights of winter there?
> Oh, strange delusion, that I did not greet
> Thy blest approach! And, Oh, to Heaven how lost,
> If my ingratitude's unkindly frost
> Has chilled the bleeding wounds upon thy feet!
> How oft my guardian angel gently cried,
> "Soul, from thy casement look, and thou shalt see
> How he persists to knock and wait for thee!"
> And, Oh! how often to that voice of sorrow,
> "To-morrow we will open," I replied,
> And when the morrow came I answered still, "To-morrow."
> (From *The Complete Poetical Works of Longfellow*, Cambridge
> Edition [Cambridge, Mass.: Riverside Press, 1922], p. 593)

Then pray: *Forgive me, Lord, for the many times I have turned down your invitation, and for the many other times in which I have accepted it lightly, thinking of coming to your great feast dressed in my rags of sin. Clothe me anew in love and holiness. Make me obedient to your command. When you send me out on the roads seeking new guests for your feast, remind me constantly that no one whom I may encounter is less worthy than I, even if they are dressed in rags. Amen.*

Sixth Day: Read Matthew 22:15-33

See: The passage may be divided in two parts, verses 15-22 and 23-33. Notice that in the first part the antagonists are the Pharisees, and in the second it is the Sadducees. The Pharisees believed in the resurrection of the dead, but the Sadducees did not. Also, while the Sadducees belonged to the higher echelons of society and openly collaborated with the Roman government, the Pharisees were closer to the people. They preferred to stay away from politics, not supporting the Roman regime but also not opposing it.

The Pharisees pose a captious question to Jesus. The Herodians to whom the text refers were people who collaborated with the Empire. If Jesus says that the tribute should not be paid, he will be accused as a subversive before the Roman authorities. If he says that it is to be paid, he will lose the support of many Jews for whom the tribute itself is a symbol of Rome's power over their nation.

Jesus' answer does not mean that politics belong to Caesar and religious matters to God. Jesus asks whose image the coin bears. It is Caesar's. This means that no matter how you think you have earned a particular coin, it is Caesar's. Do not claim then to retain in the name of God what you have actually earned serving Caesar. Although Jesus does not refer to this explicitly, a central biblical doctrine is that human beings bear the image of God. Therefore, the coin that bears Caesar's image must be returned to Caesar, and that which bears God's image (that is, human life itself) belongs to God.

Then the Sadducees seek to trap Jesus with another tricky question, showing some of the possible complications of the doctrine of resurrection. Jesus responds that they do not understand the resurrection and that in denying it they imply that God is a God of the dead, not of the living. In both cases, those who hear the answers that Jesus gives are astounded (verses 22 and 33).

Judge: Consider the phrase: "Give therefore to the emperor the things that are the emperor's, and to God the things that are God's." Does this mean that some things belong to Caesar and some others to God? Is God not the

God of all? If God is the owner of all, are we to give to God only our spiritual life? Does our body also belong to God? Our dreams and aspirations? When we have decided how to invest our time and money, must we consider God to be the owner of both? When you decide how to vote, is God also the owner of that aspect of your life?

And what then belongs to the emperor? These are the things that bear the image or imprint of other lords and not of God. Sometimes we cling to things that bear the stamp of other lords. For instance, if we have power or riches that are not in the service of God and that we cannot put in that service, the best we can do is get rid of them.

What is there in your life that does not belong to God?

Act: Consider this last question carefully. Pray: *God and Lord of my life, take this that I now render unto you. I do not know how to use it for your service. But I pray you to take it and use it. And if it cannot be used for your service, I pray that you will destroy it. For I do not wish to have anything that is not yours. Amen.*

Seventh Day: Read Matthew 22:34-46

See: Now the action shifts. For the last few days, those who have questioned Jesus have been the Pharisees, the chief priests, and the Sadducees. The same will be true at the beginning of today's text. In this case it is the Pharisees who once again try to entrap Jesus by means of a difficult question. But in the second part of the passage, Jesus takes the initiative, posing now a question that the Pharisees cannot answer.

The Pharisees' question seems simple but is not. Matthew tells us that the one posing the question was a lawyer: This man was an expert in the law of God.

Those who studied the law and classified the commandments in it had listed a total of 613. But there was some disagreement as to whether some were more important than others. Some held that to say that some commandments were more important than others was to diminish the value of those others, and that therefore, every attempt to establish an order among God's commandments was an offense against the law itself.

We have already seen some cases of apparent conflicts among the commandments in those passages where Jesus shows himself ready to break the law of the Sabbath in order to respond to a person in need. The seventh commandment was part of the law, but so was the commandment to love those in need. When such conflicts arose, one had to find a way to solve them, which is why the students of the law discussed how to order the commandments according to their importance.

Therefore, the question that this lawyer poses is not easy. At this time, many other interpreters of the law have discussed and continue discussing it without reaching an agreement. Perhaps the lawyer hopes that once the discussion gets into technical matters, Jesus will not know what to say.

Jesus gives a simple answer: "The greatest and first commandment" is to love God. This was quite an acceptable answer, for there were interpreters of the law who held that this was indeed the first of all commandments. But Jesus is not content with merely responding to the question. The lawyer asks him to say which is the first commandment, and Jesus adds which one is the second: loving your neighbor as yourself.

That is important, for there were those who, using the excuse of loving God and fulfilling all their religious obligations, did not show love for the neighbor.

Then Jesus takes the initiative, posing the question: "What do you think of the Messiah? Whose son is he?" Quoting Psalm 110, he argues that the Messiah is greater than David, who calls him "Lord." What is at stake here is whether the Messiah is merely to restore the throne of David or to fulfill a much greater mission. No one is able to respond to this argument, and the enemies of Jesus are silenced.

Judge: Jesus declares that "all the law and the prophets" hang on the two commandments of loving God and the neighbor. That means that, without obeying those two commandments, the others cannot really be obeyed.

In our churches and faith communities, we are tempted to give priority to other commandments. In some churches rules of conduct are established, and whoever does not follow them is treated without mercy. There are churches in which if a member goes to the movies on a Sunday, that is enough for all to begin gossiping. What is worse: going to a movie on a Sunday or speaking ill of a neighbor? Think about your own faith community. Are there rules in it that seem to be higher than the love of God and neighbor? What are they?

Act: Write down those rules that exist in your community. Across from them, copy the two commandments of love that Jesus mentions in today's passage. Memorize them. Whenever you feel inclined to condemn someone, to think or to speak ill of someone, repeat these commandments to yourself. Then, ask yourself if what you are about to say or to do obeys those commandments. If not, do not say it or do it.

For Group Study

The group may begin their discussion remembering some of the passages that have been studied in which someone accused Jesus of not obeying the commandment regarding the day of rest. The group may analyze those passages in the light of what Jesus says here about the first two commandments. Having done that, continue the discussion making a list of some of the laws, rules, and practices that may seem to be most important in your church or faith community. Write that list on a large sheet of paper so that all can continue reading it.

Now ask if it is possible for these rules sometimes to conflict with the commandments of love.

End the session by all repeating out loud the two commandments of love. Invite the group to give each other signs of mutual love (a handshake, a hug, a greeting, a good word, and so forth).

W E E K
ELEVEN

First Day: Read Matthew 23:1-12

See: On the whole, chapter 23 seems to be a single speech by Jesus; however, it can be divided into three parts. The first (verses 1-12) is addressed "to the crowds and to his disciples." The second (verses 13-36) is a series of "woes" against the scribes and Pharisees. Finally, beginning with verse 37, Jesus addresses Jerusalem. The common thread that runs through all three parts of the speech is the infidelity of the religious leaders of Jerusalem, and in particular, of the scribes and Pharisees.

In his warnings "to the crowds and to his disciples," Jesus does not condemn the teachings of the scribes and Pharisees. On the contrary, he tells his listeners that they must do what those leaders tell them but not what they themselves do. The evil is not in what the scribes and Pharisees say but in what they do, and that for two reasons: (1) because they load others with burdens and obligations which they themselves do not carry and (2) because they seek to be praised and respected for their religiosity and to receive titles of particular prestige and respect.

Jesus tells his followers that they must reject all of this. Much of what he says here is a reiteration of what we already saw when studying the Sermon on the Mount about not boasting when giving alms, when praying, or when fasting. Instead of such an attitude (which characterizes the scribes and Pharisees, for they want to be first, great, and important), among the disciples of Jesus, the greatest will be the one who serves, for "all who exalt themselves will be humbled, and all who humble themselves will be exalted."

Judge: Do we in the church obey what Jesus commands his disciples in this passage? Is it true that among us the greatest is the one who serves? Do we not like to give each other high-sounding titles and honors and to boast of all our holiness? As you observe the attitudes of the church toward the rest of the world, do you think that the church will be praised for having humbled itself, or will it be humbled for having exalted itself?

Act: From this point forward, whenever someone asks how a particular decision will affect the prestige of the church, remind the group that the purpose of the church is not to claim prestige but to serve and to give witness. Suggest the possibility that the church must humble itself in order to have God exalt it.

Make a firm resolution to render some service that others do not wish to render because it is not acknowledged or respected.

Second Day: Read Matthew 23:13-36

See: Today's passage is part of a series of "woes" against the scribes and Pharisees. Verses 13-16, 23, 25, 27, and 29 begin with the words "woe to you." In most of these, Jesus calls the scribes and Pharisees "hypocrites." Let us study those "woes" to see what is the nature of the hypocrisy Jesus condemns.

Verse 13 accuses the scribes and Pharisees of creating obstacles for admission into the kingdom of heaven, while they themselves do not enter.

Verse 14 (which does not appear in some versions, including the NRSV) accuses them of abuse and injustice. To "devour widow's houses" means to exploit them and leave them without resources. And then, to make matters worse, the scribes and Pharisees cover their abuse with pious and long prayers.

Verse 15 accuses them of seeking to convert others and then not really leading them to God but rather to hell.

Verses 16-22 accuses them of giving more importance to the gold in the Temple than to the Temple itself, of being more concerned with the offering than with the God to whom the offering is presented.

Verses 23-24 declare that they are too concerned over the details of the law and not over that which is most important; that they carry detailed accounts in order to tithe even for the most insignificant, and then forget the "weightier matters of the law: justice and mercy and faith." This is likened to straining a gnat but swallowing a camel. (Remember that the camel was the biggest animal in the area.)

Verses 25-26 and 27-28 accuse the scribes and Pharisees of an outward purity while within them there is rottenness and uncleanness.

Finally, verses 29-35 accuse them of condemning their own ancestors who persecuted the prophets, when they themselves are no different and are about to do the same.

The passage ends with verse 36, where the word "generation" is probably to be understood not in the sense of all the people born at about the same time but rather in the sense of a group, family, or line of descendants. (In 23:33 the phrase "brood of vipers" means "family of vipers.")

Judge: Begin with the last of the "woes," which warns us that we are not to think that we are all that different from our ancestors. If we believe that we would never do such a thing, let us remember that this was also the belief of the scribes and the Pharisees about those who before them killed and persecuted the prophets and the just.

Then, in the light of this last point, examine each of the "woes" in order to see to what degree it applies to us and to our churches. For instance, is it possible that we are too concerned about details, while we swallow the camel of injustice and of lack of mercy? Is it possible that we may be more concerned about the finances of the church than about the will of God? Is it possible that our evangelism is simply a way of gaining members without really leading them to the reign of God?

Act: Write in your notebook a new series of "woes," but begin each of them by saying *Woe is me.* Then, write something similar to what Jesus says, but relate it to your life and your faith (for instance, you could write: *Woe is me, for I am so concerned about my own prayers but do nothing for the needy!*) In prayer, bring to God what you have written, asking for forgiveness and newness of life.

Third Day: Read Matthew 23:37–24:2

See: Jesus continues speaking, but now he is addressing the city of Jerusalem rather than the disciples, the crowd in general, or the scribes and Pharisees, as in the text that we studied yesterday.

Jerusalem is the highest expression of what we have repeatedly seen in the Gospel of Matthew: that those who were at the edge are placed at the center, and what was at the center may become marginal. Jerusalem is the holy city, where the Temple stands, and as such has a very important place in the heart of Jesus. But Jerusalem is also the capital city, the center of both religious and political power. It is in Jerusalem that the most important priests live, as well as the most famous scribes and the leading Pharisees, many of whom have turned religion into something ever more difficult and complicated, and this for their own benefit. Therefore, Jesus loves Jerusalem but at the same time sees the enormous contradiction of a holy city that "kills the prophets and stones those who are sent to it" (verse 37).

The image of a hen that gathers her brood is particularly tender, and it shows that Jesus does not hate Jerusalem but is pained by its hardness of heart and its sad destiny. He also knows that eventually the city itself will repeat what his disciples said when he entered it: "Blessed is the one who comes in the name of the Lord" (21:9)!

The moral and religious tragedy crystallizes around the Temple. Jesus does not condemn the Temple. But when his disciples speak enthusiastically about its wonderful buildings, Jesus tells them "not one stone will be left here upon another" (24:2).

Judge: It is very easy to read this passage as if it referred only to the hardness of the heart of Jerusalem and of the leaders of Israel who lived and ruled in it. But it is important to remember that the Bible is also the word of God for us. Therefore, we have to ask ourselves not only what those people did almost twenty centuries ago but also, and above all, what it tells us.

When we look at the matter in this fashion we see that we too run the risk of being found wanting. If we imagine that God loves us more than the rest of humankind, or that we are special, or that we deserve certain privileges simply because we are believers, let us take care lest Jesus will pronounce over ourselves and over our church words similar to his lament over Jerusalem.

For instance, we all like to show pride over our churches and their ministry. There certainly is a place for this. It would be sad to have to be constantly ashamed of our churches and what they do. It is thanks to those communities that we can live as Christians in today's world, and it is through those communities that much of the work of God is done. But if we come to the conclusion that our large, beautiful building or our donations to missionaries have assured our place in God's reign, it is time to take heed.

Our place is assured in God's reign not because of something we have done or will do but rather because of what Jesus Christ has already done.

Act: If Jesus acted as he did in spite of Jerusalem's faithlessness and if Jesus acts toward us as he does in spite of our own faithlessness, we cannot but act likewise toward others. Think of the community around you in church as a scattered brood. What can the church do in order to shelter them under its wings? Write down your reflections and share them with others in your congregation.

Fourth Day: Read Matthew 24:3-51 *11-28-04*

See: Today's passage is long, but its meaning is clear. The disciples wish to know when will be the end of the age, the time when Jesus will return; and Jesus tells them that they cannot know this. Furthermore, he warns them that there will be many false prophets claiming that they are the Christ and that there will also be many who will try to foretell the final consummation.

Jesus warns his disciples that they have to be constantly ready for that final moment because they will never know when it will be. The Lord will come "as the lightning comes from the east and flashes as far as the west" (verse 27). This means that he will come without allowing for last-minute preparations. That is the meaning of the section beginning in verse 16. By then it will be too late to remedy what has been done or to turn back.

Toward the end of the passage, the theme is affirmed with two other images. The first is that of a thief who comes when he is not expected (verses 42-44). The thief does not announce his arrival but rather seeks to take those who are in the house by surprise, and therefore comes when he is least expected. If that were not the case, he could not steal. The second image is that of the owner of a house who went away and left a servant in charge of his goods (verses 45-51). The owner will return without giving warning. If he arrives and finds that the servant, even though not forewarned, has kept everything in order, the owner will give him greater authority. But if the servant makes use of the owner's absence in order to abuse his power, "the master of that slave will come on a day when he does not expect him and at an hour that he does not know. He will cut him in pieces and put him with the hypocrites, where there will be weeping and gnashing of teeth."

The common thread joining these three images (the lightning, the thief, and the absent master) is the unexpected arrival of the Lord.

Judge: One of the favorite occupations of some Christians is attempting to predict the date of the Lord's return. That has been the case for many centuries, and obviously every prediction has been wrong. Those who foretold the date in the past erred, and those who foretell it today also err, for Jesus says very clearly that he will come as lightning, like a thief at night, or like an owner who unexpectedly returns home.

Do you know someone who is trying to predict the coming of the Lord? Have you heard over the radio or seen on television someone who has been predicting the coming? What does this passage tell us about such predictions?

Act: Make a firm resolution to reject any doctrine or theory that claims to say when, where, or how the Lord will come. At the same time, make a resolution to live in such a way that you will always be ready for the Lord's coming, just in case it happens at that particular time. Think of your life as a house whose owner has given you to watch. What will you tell the owner if he suddenly arrives? Write down your reflections.

Fifth Day: Read Matthew 25:1-13

See: The parable of the ten bridesmaids continues on the same subject: The reign of God comes unexpectedly, and there will be no time to prepare for it. The story itself is simple: Five wise and five foolish bridesmaids are expecting the bridegroom for a wedding feast. The five wise ones prepare for waiting, taking with them not only the lamps they will need to light their way but also the oil they will need for a possible long wait. The five foolish ones only take their lamps. The bridegroom is delayed, and he arrives unexpectedly at midnight. The wise ones still have oil for their lamps and prepare to receive the bridegroom. But the others, who have used up all their oil while watching at an earlier hour, have to go looking for more and miss the feast.

The point of the parable is explicitly told in verse 13: "Keep awake therefore, for you know neither the day nor the hour."

Judge: We have heard what was said yesterday: the bridegroom would come unexpectedly. But now there is the added dimension of waiting. If the bridegroom had come when he was expected, the foolish bridesmaids would have had no problem. But he was delayed, and when he arrived he was not expected.

Sometimes what makes waiting most difficult is its length. When that happens, it is quite easy to forget what one is awaiting. The foolish bridesmaids had enough oil at the beginning, but spent it all while waiting, having none at the necessary moment.

How can we remain alert for the fulfillment of the promises of the reign of God when we do not know how this will happen? Think for instance about sports. You are sitting in the dugout. You do not know when you will be called. Perhaps you will not play for weeks. But when you are called, you better be ready to play. What do you do in order to be ready? You exercise just as if you were playing. You practice. Perhaps that is what Christians have to do: live as if we were already in the reign of God, practicing for it so that when it comes we shall be ready.

Act: Look at your life as a practice for God's reign. Write down some of the characteristics of that reign, and consider how you can prepare for it. These characteristics could be things such as love, peace, justice, and so forth. For instance, how can you practice now for a reign of love?

Jot down your reflections.

Sixth Day: Read Matthew 25:14-30

See: This is the well-known parable of the talents. As we have already seen, a talent was an enormous amount of money, approximately what a laborer would earn in fifteen years of work. Therefore, an element of the parable that we sometimes do not notice is that the owner was very liberal in what he left the servants. It was not simply, as we may think, that he left five coins to one, two to the second, and only one to the third. Even the third steward received a respectable sum.

Note also that the owner leaves. This is a frequent theme in the parables of Jesus: The owner is absent; he goes to a distant land and leaves others in charge. It is precisely the absence of the owner that gives the servants particular responsibility.

When the owner returns, he expects not simply that each servant will have taken care of what he has received but rather that he will have employed it as the owner himself would have done. Therefore, the timid servant who received a single talent is condemned, not because he did not take care of it but because he did not use it.

Judge: In our everyday language we employ the word *talent* meaning something we can do well (things such as singing, preaching, or teaching).

But the "talents" here represent everything we have received from the owner. This includes not only things that we can do well but also money, power, and life itself. God has given us all of these things so that we may use them according to the divine will and make them prosper.

The subject of the absence of the master is important. It is by reason of that absence that the servants are in charge of the talents. Sometimes we wish that God would be more clearly manifest in our days, intervening more directly and fixing everything. But God does not do it. It is almost as if God were absent. What we do not always see is that God's apparent absence has turned us into stewards of what God has given us. As long as God is not openly manifested in God's reign, we are responsible for all that we have received. It is precisely because God does not solve every problem or destroy every injustice that we are God's stewards, like those servants of the absent master.

But the apparent absence does not mean lack of interest. In the parable, the owner returns in order to judge what each servant did with the talents he had received. What will the owner say when the time comes to decide about the use that we have made of what we have received?

Act: Think about something that you have, that until this moment you have not considered placing at the service of God. It may be a free lunch hour at noon. It can be one of those things we usually call *talents,* such as singing, speaking, writing, visiting the sick, teaching, caring for children, and so forth. Whatever it might be, think about how to place it at God's service. Pray that God will help you to discover the talent you may have buried, perhaps even unwittingly.

Seventh Day: Read Matthew 25:31-46

See: This is a dramatic passage. It presents an image of the final judgment: Jesus is seated on his throne in the presence of all humankind, separating people into two groups—one to his right and the other to his left.

The image of separating sheep from goats may surprise us. Yet, it would be a common event at that time, when people raised both sheep and goats and often would shepherd a herd in which both kinds of animals were together. At various times (for instance, when the sheep were to be sheared for wool) they would be separated.

Jesus tells those on his right they are blessed, for they will inherit the reign of God; and the others are told that they have been condemned.

Each group receives an explanation. The measure is the same for both. It has to do with the manner in which each dealt with Jesus: Those who fed him when he was hungry or visited him when he was in prison are blessed and will inherit the reign. Those who did not do so will be condemned.

This is a surprising measure for judgment. Jesus does not tell those on his right that they are to inherit the kingdom because they were religious or because they believed in him. He does not tell those on his left that they are condemned because they did not belong to the right church. Jesus says that each is to be tried on the basis of the manner in which each dealt with him. It has nothing to do with orthodoxy or with believing the right doctrine.

It is not only we who are surprised but also those who are present in the story: "Lord, when was it that we saw you...?" Those who were serving Jesus did not know that they were doing so. Those who did not were also ignorant of that fact.

The answer, both to the blessed and the cursed, is the same: "Truly I tell you, just as you did it [or did not do it] to one of the least of these who are members of my family, you did it to me [or you did not do it to me]." But the time of judgment is too late to undo what has been done. Therefore, the passage ends with the awesome words: "These will go away into eternal punishment, but the righteous into eternal life."

Judge: Here, Jesus gives his disciples some indications as to how they are to serve in the future, when he is no longer physically with them. That also is our situation. Sometimes we think if we had Jesus right here by us, telling us what we are to do, Christian life would be much easier. The truth is that Jesus has told us clearly what we must do. In order to serve him today, we must serve those who are in need.

In studying the list of those whom Jesus tells us to serve, we note that they are people who usually don't have anyone to serve them. That is once again one of the central themes of the teaching of Jesus: The last are to be first, and the least are the greatest in the kingdom. Jesus himself, who did not have a place to lay his head, is a living example of this. In this strange reign of God, the king does not present himself dwelling in palaces, with crowns of jewels, but as a stranger with a crown of thorns. Likewise, those who wish to be servants of such a king must be ready to serve, not the powerful, but the hungry, the naked, the alien, the ill, the prisoners.

This means that service to the neighbor in need is not an option in Christian life. It is not something else we could do. It is not that those Christians who wish to be more devoted should visit the sick and feed the hungry. According to the passage, those who refuse the hungry are refusing to feed Jesus. That is, it is impossible to be a faithful Christian without serving those whom Jesus calls "the least of these who are members of my family."

In the church one often hears debates about whether religious life or social service is most important. This passage tells us that the discussion itself is wrong. They are not two different matters; they are a single reality. The Jesus we worship in church is the same Jesus whom we serve in the neighbor. To make these into two different options is to deny Jesus and his words.

Neither lack of resources nor lack of time is a sufficient excuse. Even those of us who have limited resources can always find something that we can share with others. If we have more than that, then our obligation is even greater.

According to the passage, those who are present at the final judgment are surprised when they learn they have served Jesus or that they have refused to serve him. That surprise is perfectly understood, for most people think that salvation is to be attained through a magical formula or believing certain points of doctrine. But those of us who are Christian do not even have such an excuse. We have been given fair warning: We are to serve Jesus by feeding the hungry and serving the needy.

Act: First, decide from now on to avoid any contrast or competition between devotion and social service or between preaching and feeding the hungry. The two are of a piece, and if you neglect one of them, both suffer.

Second, since the passage speaks of concrete needs, determine what you are going to do during the next twenty-four hours in order to serve Jesus. Can you visit someone who is lonely? Can you feed someone who for whatever reason lacks adequate nutrition? What will you do? Write it down, and commit yourself in prayer.

For Group Study

After studying the passage, discuss who the needy are in the community—those who have fewest resources.

Then ask: *What do they need?* Note that in the Bible passage, each human need requires different and specific answers: food for the hungry, welcome and shelter for the alien, clothing for the naked. Therefore, it is not enough to say: *They need Jesus Christ* or *They need faith.* They certainly need that, as we all do, but here we are speaking of specific needs.

The second question is *what resources do we have that we can use as a response to their need?* In responding, encourage the group to take account both of their own personal and congregational resources and those of the wider church (resources that we can request through proper channels).

Finally, ask: *If there are people in need and we have resources with which to respond, what will the Lord say on the Day of Judgment? Are we meeting those needs in such a way that he will tell us, "Come, you that are blessed by my Father, inherit the kingdom prepared for you"* (25:34)?

W E E K
TWELVE

First Day: Read Matthew 26:1-16

See: The time of the trial and crucifixion is approaching. Jesus knows this, and he tells his disciples. The leaders of the people ("the chief priests and the elders of the people") also know it. Toward the end of the passage, Judas knows it in a particular way, for he has sold himself to the chief priests for thirty pieces of silver.

Jesus is, as usual, with unlikely people, "in the house of Simon the leper," when a woman comes to him. She must be rich, for she has a jar of very expensive perfume—and at that time, as today, good perfumes could command a very high price. Certainly, her liberality approaches the extravagant, for rather than perfuming Jesus with a few drops, which would suffice, she pours the jar over his head.

The more pragmatic disciples are shocked. So much money! Wouldn't it have been better to sell the perfume and give the money to the poor? But Jesus comes out in defense of the woman. "You always have the poor with you, but you will not always have me," he tells them, and he adds that the woman has anointed his body for burial and that wherever the gospel is preached, what she has done will be told.

Judge: The phrase "you always have the poor with you" has been used to claim that Christians are not to be concerned with poverty, for it is the will of God. Do you think that is really what Jesus meant? This phrase is a quotation of Deuteronomy 15:11, where God tells Israel that, if the people were faithful and practiced justice, there would be no poor in the midst of them; but, since they will not do the will of God, there will always be poor among them. Therefore, poverty is the result of the disobedience and injustice of society and not of God's design.

Think about another way of understanding this text. Jesus is telling his disciples that what this woman has done is justified because he is still in their midst and is preparing to die. But when he is no longer with them, the poor will still be there, and then will be the time to sell jars of expensive perfume in order to give to the poor. Thus, what Jesus is saying is not that we should not be concerned for the poor but exactly the opposite: We must show a liberality toward them similar to that of the woman with the perfume.

Act: Have you ever performed an a̲c̲t̲ o̲f̲ l̲i̲b̲e̲r̲a̲l̲i̲t̲y̲ that verged on the extravagant, as the woman in this story? Is there perhaps right now a jar of expensive perfume, something that you truly do not need, which could be better used? What might Jesus wish you to do with it? Place it in prayer at the feet of Jesus, and do whatever you are told.

Second Day: Read Matthew 26:17-29

See: The words of the institution of the Lord's Supper are well known. However, we often forget their context. In reading this passage, we see that the time was not easy. Jesus prepares for this particular meal in a way that appears mysterious. He sends his disciples ahead to prepare the place, but he does not go. This may just be a precaution, for Jesus knows that there is a conspiracy to kill him. In the passage studied yesterday, we are told that Judas has already made the necessary arrangements to betray him. During the meal itself Jesus tells them that one of them will indeed betray him. Finally, he tells them that it will be Judas. One can only imagine the tenseness of the situation, the fear and mistrust among the disciples.

In the midst of that situation, and amidst all dangers, conspiracies, tensions, and alarms of that night, Jesus takes the bread and the cup, gives them to his disciples, tells them that he is to be betrayed, and turns that bread and that cup into his response to the challenges of that fateful night.

Judge: In our churches we regularly celebrate the Lord's Supper. Sometimes we think that in order to celebrate it worthily we must make certain that we do it in a tranquil atmosphere, without thinking about anything that might cause us distraction or concern. But when Jesus first celebrated it, it was not in such a tranquil situation. He knew that one of his disciples had sold him, and the result would be his passion and death. It was in the midst of such circumstances that Jesus established the Lord's

Supper. It is precisely for such circumstances that the Lord's Supper is most valuable.

In the midst of the night, that dinner was Jesus' challenge to the powers of evil. It was also an announcement that, in spite of those powers and in spite of the sufferings of the cross, he would finally triumph. That is why he says: "I tell you, I will never again drink of this fruit of the vine until that day when I drink it new with you in my Father's kingdom."

Act: Make it a point of participating in the Lord's Supper whenever it is celebrated in your church. When you do so, bring all your concerns to the table of the Lord. They will never be worse or more than those of that first night of betrayal. The Lord's Supper will remind you that you are to eat and drink with him in God's reign, and will give you strength to continue along the way until that glorious day.

Third Day: Read Matthew 26:30-35

See: The change in attitude on the part of the disciples is surprising. During the supper, when Jesus declared that one of them would betray him, they all asked: "Surely not I, Lord?" This means that they were not quite sure of themselves. But now their attitude is different. Jesus tells them that they will all abandon him. Peter—fiery and impulsive Peter—disagrees: "Though all become deserters because of you, I will never desert you." Jesus tells him that before the cock crows Peter will deny him three times. But Peter insists, and Jesus seems to let the matter stand until events would convince Peter. Note also that, although the text speaks specifically about Peter, it adds: "And so said all the disciples."

Judge: Why do you think Peter and the rest were so sure of themselves? Could it be because they did not understand the terrible events about to occur? Could it be because they thought themselves to be stronger and more courageous than they really were? Have you ever had the experience of having been quite sure of yourself then suddenly failing and falling without knowing how or why?

In whom do you trust for your safety and firmness? In your own strength? One's own strength is not enough before the powers of evil. In your own faith? Not even faith, as something that you have, will keep you firm. In the power of God? Only that power is greater than all the rest. Only God will be able to support you in times of real trial.

Act: Pray: *Forgive me, Lord, for the many times in which trusting in my own strength I have failed you. You know me better than I know myself. You are closer to me than I myself. In times of trial, give me your strength to be a victor. Do not allow me to fall. If I do fall, take me by the hand and raise me up. For Jesus, my Lord and Savior of the fallen. Amen.*

Fourth Day: Read Matthew 26:36-46 ᒋ-ᔔ0-O5

See: This is one of the most dramatic passages in the entire Gospel. Knowing that the time is near, Jesus goes to a secluded place to pray. Alone with the Father, he pleads that, if it is possible, he may be spared the suffering of the cross. But he also adds that what is to be done is not his will, but the Father's.

At Gethsemane, Jesus leaves everyone else behind, telling his disciples that he is going to pray. He takes three of those closest to him: Peter and the two sons of Zebedee. But even these are left behind when Jesus goes to pray alone. Not even these three are aware of the anguish of the moment. Upon returning, Jesus finds them sleeping. He scolds them for not having remained awake with him in the midst of his anguish, and he goes back to pray. Once again, he finds them asleep, and he tells them that they must stay awake and pray with him. Finally, after a third period of prayer, when he has come to the conclusion that the bitter cup of the passion will not pass him by, he returns and tells them that now they can sleep, for "the hour is at hand, and the Son of Man is betrayed into the hands of sinners."

Judge: The passage points us in at least two directions. The first has to do with Jesus himself. Quite often, because we know that he is divine, we forget that he is also a human being like us. We imagine that Jesus did not suffer anguish and uncertainty. We think that Jesus faced life and its trials with an unmovable calm. But the text tells us quite the opposite. Jesus suffered just as we do. Just as our sufferings include both mental anguish and physical pain, Jesus suffered both: the anguish of Gethsemane and the physical pain of his passion and death.

This is important, for a crucial element of the biblical message is that, through Jesus, God has become one of us in order to participate in our lives and redeem them. Without sharing in human pain, Jesus would not have redeemed it. Now we know that God is compassionate toward our pain and understands it, for in Jesus, God suffered as we do.

This leads us to the second important point in this biblical text: the manner in which we ourselves are to face our own pain. Jesus does not deny his pain or his anguish. Yet, some Christians believe that they have to be better than Jesus. They think that confessing their anxieties would be proclaiming a lack of faith. They think that success, peace, and happiness are a proof of their own virtue and of God's favor. But even Jesus suffered pain and anguish. Therefore, to claim that we do not share in this is the same as claiming that somehow we are above Jesus.

Act: Jesus places his will at the service of the Father's will: "not what I want but what you want." That is what Christians are called to do. It is not a matter of not suffering nor even of demanding from God that we be spared suffering. It is a matter of frankly telling God as well as others that we suffer, that we are anguished, that we wish that our burden would be eased. Think about your own sufferings and anguish. Place them before God. End your prayer with the words: Yet not what I want but what you want.

3-20-05

Fifth Day: Read Matthew 26:47-56

See: The action takes place immediately after the anguished prayer in Gethsemane. Yesterday's passage ended with the words: "See, my betrayer is at hand." Today's passage begins: "While he was still speaking . . . "

Those who arrive are Judas and a large crowd with swords and clubs. Apparently, while Jesus was praying in Gethsemane, Judas went and told those who had conspired with him that Jesus and his disciples were in a secluded place. (The reason a traitor was necessary was that the chief priests and their accomplices feared that if they arrested Jesus when he was teaching, there would be a riot or at least some disorder. Therefore, they needed someone to tell them when Jesus would be alone or nearly so.)

Those who come with swords and clubs are neither soldiers nor the official police. That is why they come armed as best they can. They come "from the chief priests and the elders of the people." Although it is the powerful in Jerusalem who conspire against Jesus, they do not come forward. They stay in Jerusalem and send in their place a crowd that may have been bought.

The sign by which the crowd would know Jesus was a kiss from Judas. When Judas kisses him, Jesus is quite aware of what he is doing, and still he calls him "friend"!

There is an attempt at resistance among those who accompany Jesus, with the result that one of those who has come to arrest him loses an ear. But Jesus orders his attempted defender to put away his sword, for he does not need it. Indeed, he could even ask the Father to send legions of angels. He looks at those who have come to arrest him and reminds them that they did not arrest him when he was teaching openly at the Temple, and now they come with swords and clubs. There is an implied accusation here of cowardice and injustice. But in spite of that, Jesus does not rebel but simply goes with them.

It was then, according to the text, that all the disciples deserted him and fled, thus fulfilling what Jesus had told them would happen and what they had insisted would not.

Judge: Much could be said about this passage, which has been included in the history of humankind as one of its most infamous episodes. So much so, that the name of *Judas* has become a synonym for *traitor.* That name has been abandoned and now hardly anyone would dare bear it. But the infamy of Judas sometimes hides two other infamies from us. One of them—the flight of the disciples—Jesus himself had foretold. We shall return to an aspect of it in two days when we deal with Peter's denial.

The other infamy is less visible in the account but is no less real. The chief priests and the elders of Israel, the people who were supposed to be teachers and models of virtue and integrity, conspire to arrest and kill a teacher who does not make them appear in a very positive light. When the time comes for action, they are not the ones who actually carry it out but send, instead, a crowd armed with clubs and swords.

This is a common phenomenon. Those who are in power decide to commit a crime or an infamy, but they do not wish it to be known that they are the ones behind what is taking place. Therefore, they use their power and their money to send others in their stead to do what they themselves dare not do.

What happens in the field of secular life sometimes happens even in the church. We do not get to the point of ordering someone else killed, but there are some who manage to hurt others by starting rumors with the hope that the name of the one who did it will never be known.

Act: Have you ever done indirect damage to anyone? In that case, pray for forgiveness from God as well as from that person, if at all possible. Remember also that sometimes much indirect damage is done unwittingly (that is, that what we have done is hidden not only from others but even from ourselves). That may be the case, for instance, when we repeat a rumor about someone. At times, we criticize for the mere pleasure of it without thinking about the pain that we may produce. We speak without measuring our words, and what we say eventually harms another. Make a commitment to measure your actions, always thinking of their possible consequences for others.

3 20 -05   *Sixth Day: Read Matthew 26:57-68*

See: This is the beginning of what has usually been called the "trial" of Jesus. But it is important to understand that this is not really the trial that will eventually condemn him to death. The Jewish council did not have authority to decree the death penalty, which could only be ordered by the Roman governor.

What takes place at the council is a religious trial. Those who are present are only the members of the council, particularly "the high priests and the elders of the people." They are gathered at the house of the high priest, Caiaphas. Therefore, this is not a matter of crowds. What is more, in the courtyard of Caiaphas there are few people, for Peter can go in and sit there.

The false witnesses do not achieve much. Their most serious accusation is that Jesus has said he can destroy the Temple and build it again in three days. Such an accusation would suffice to provoke the anger of many Jews, but much more was needed. It is at this point that Caiaphas asks Jesus directly if he is the Messiah, and Jesus responds, finally accepting that title.

On hearing those words, Caiaphas tears his clothes (a sign of pain and shame) and declares that Jesus has committed blasphemy. As a response to that, the council declares that he deserves death. At that point the meeting ends in a sort of riot, for some spit on Jesus and strike him. Mocking him, they hit him and ask him as a prophet to tell them who it was that struck him.

Judge: Since we know that the council did not have the power to declare the death penalty, what we see in all of these actions of mocking Jesus is the wrath of those who feel impotent. Throughout the entire story of the conflict between Jesus and the leaders of Israel, it is clear that the latter have no real power and that whatever power they have depends on

Roman support. This is why they fear that Jesus' preaching will lead to a riot, which in turn will provoke a Roman intervention. Therefore, their fury against Jesus is, in a way, fury against those whom they do not dare attack. Because they themselves are oppressed and do not wish to acknowledge it, they oppress Jesus in order to feel strong and courageous. Have you seen something similar in other cases? A typical case would be that of a child who, because his or her parents will not give in to his or her wants, oppresses a younger sibling. But there are many other cases, which we witness daily. For instance, a second-level employee of a company, frustrated because he cannot ascend higher, begins abusing those who are under his authority. Injustice begets injustice, and oppression begets oppression.

Act: Is someone oppressing you? Begin by acknowledging it, for sometimes we do not even dare tell ourselves that we are oppressed. Then, try to free yourself from that oppression. Have no doubt: God does not like oppression.

There are several solutions that you may employ in order to try to be free from oppression. In many cases, it is best simply to tell the person who is oppressing you what is taking place, and ask for a change. In other cases, it is necessary to find other persons who are similarly oppressed, and create a group of solidarity and support that may help you in your struggle. No matter what the case, it is important that, as a person of faith, you act without seeking revenge and without hatred.

But that is only one side of the coin. It is important for you to ask yourself whether (perhaps as a result of your own oppression) you are oppressing others. It was such a secondhand oppression that the members of the council practiced with Jesus.

Write down your reflections. Share them with other people in similar conditions.

Seventh Day: Read Matthew 26:69-75   3 - 20 -05

See: The passage is known as "Peter's denial." Here what Jesus had foretold Peter is fulfilled. As you remember, just before the prayer in Gethsemane, Jesus told his disciples they would all desert him, and Peter as well as the rest refused to accept such a possibility. At that time Jesus told Peter: "Truly I tell you, this very night, before the cock crows, you will deny me three times" (verse 34).

When reading this passage and learning of Peter's triple denial, it is easy to forget that at least Peter did not flee with the rest of the disciples. He actually followed from a distance, "in order to see how this would end" (verse 58). When Jesus was taken to the house of Caiaphas, Peter sat in the courtyard with the guards.

Peter's denial is threefold, as Jesus had foretold. The first denial takes place when the maid says that he has been with Jesus. Although the accusation seems to have been made in private, the denial is public, for the text says that Peter "denied it before all of them, saying, 'I do not know what you are talking about.'" The second accusation comes from another servant girl but is now more public, for he speaks "to the bystanders." This second time Peter denies it even more strongly, "with an oath," he swears: "I do not know the man." The third accusation does not come from a single person, but from several, "the bystanders," who accuse Peter of being one of the followers of Jesus. This third time his response is even more vehement, for he not only denies but even curses.

Matthew tells us that "at that moment the cock crowed." At the very moment of that strongest denial, with oaths and curses, Peter hears the cock crowing and remembers the words of Jesus. It is then that he goes "out" (that is, leaves the courtyard) and weeps bitterly.

As we have noted earlier, one of the factors at play in the entire history of the passion is the opinion of the Judeans (that is, people from Judea itself) about Galileans. There was a strong pagan presence in Galilee, and therefore the Judeans spoke of it as "Galilee of the Gentiles" (4:15). The Judeans see the Galileans as only somewhat Jewish. Galileans are not deemed to be as pure as Judeans, nor do they keep the laws as strictly; and they certainly do not attend ceremonies in the Temple as often as Judeans. Therefore, when they speak of Jesus as a "Galilean" or as from "Nazareth," this has a pejorative tone. One of the manners in which Galileans were known was that they did not speak exactly the way Judeans did. They had a distinctive accent. Those in Jerusalem thought and claimed that Galileans did not know how to speak correctly. That is why the last accusation against Peter of being "one of them" is based on his accent.

What all of this indicates is that part of what is taking place during the week of the passion is a manifestation of the long-standing conflict between Judeans and these Galileans who have now arrived at the capital city claiming to have a message for all of Israel. From the point of view of Jerusalem, these Galileans are latecomers, people who do not even rightly know the law and the faith of Israel. Now these Galileans come to tell them, the true and stricter Jews, how it is that one is to please and serve God.

Judge: It is easy to read this passage, as well as the entire passion narrative, without becoming aware of the ethnic and cultural conflict that is part of the context of the events narrated. I remember a sermon that I heard many years ago, when I was still a child, in which a preacher asked himself how it was that all of these people knew that Peter was one of the disciples of Jesus. His answer was that when one has been with Jesus, it shows on your face; your face shines with peace and joy. I remember that after the sermon I sat on the curb across from church gazing at the faces of all the people leaving the church and deciding that no one had been with Jesus!

It was only years later, when I was teaching in Puerto Rico, that this text gained new meaning for me. I had been invited to preach in a church in Maryland. It was to be on Maundy Thursday, and the assigned text was Peter's denial. It was the first time I was to preach in English to a large congregation. I was concerned that my accent would make me difficult to understand. It was then that, reading this passage, I first noted that one of the ways that Judeans recognized the disciples of Jesus was by their accent. It was from that starting point, reading the Gospels again, that I began to see to what extent ethnic conflict and prejudices were at play in the confrontation between Jesus and the authorities, and eventually with the population itself, of Jerusalem.

All that has just been said about the manner in which Judeans regarded Galileans reminds us of many other ethnic and cultural conflicts in today's world. Mexican American theologian Virgilio Elizondo has commented that his experience growing up in Texas, and being Mexican in origin, is similar to that of the ancient Galileans. Being born in the United States, he is as much a citizen of the nation as anyone else; but still in Texas he is called a Mexican. On the other hand, when he goes to Mexico he is considered a foreigner from the U.S.

Have you experienced any of these issues in the life of the church? If you are a member of an ethnic minority and belong to one of the major denominations in the United States, you will know that we are commonly accepted, even encouraged, up to a certain point but not beyond that. All churches seek to attract Latinos, Asians, African Americans, and other minorities. But at the same time they fear that such a population may prove to be a problem.

Such a situation leads to insecurity. Peter is insecure, for it is quite possible that what is happening to Jesus will also happen to him. He is insecure because he is a Galilean and cannot hide it. Therefore he swears and curses as if reality could be changed by stronger words.

For minorities in the U.S., the experience of being like a Galilean, belonging only halfway, often leads to insecurity and fear. One possible consequence of such feelings is negation. We deny what we are. We wish to disappear into the dominant culture. Another, and apparently contradictory, consequence is that some try to establish a clear distinction between themselves and others.

On the other hand, quite often, among the dominant society, all kinds of other issues, prejudices, and stereotypes are used to make sure that ethnic minorities, while perhaps making some progress, stay generally in their place. Like Galileans, who are considered Jewish but not as good as the Judeans, we are admitted into society and church but only up to a certain point.

All of this leads to denial of identity and of reality both on the part of minorities and on the part of the majority. Denial is always dangerous. In denying Jesus, Peter was denying himself and his own identity. In denying ourselves and our own identity, or others and their identity, we may be denying Jesus.

Act: For several weeks we have been noting the need to be committed in service to those in need around us. You have been reflecting on your own experiences in seeking to serve such people. Also, it is quite possible that in many cases you have found this rather difficult.

Ask yourself: *Am I perhaps denying my relationship with some people, as if they were quite different from myself? When it is difficult for me to relate to them, could it be that I see my own reflection in them, and fear that I might be like them?*

Remember however that Peter went and wept bitterly and that his repentance was acceptable to the Lord. Likewise, if you have denied the Lord, or if you have denied him in the needy around you, the way to repentance is still open.

Pray: *Lord, you have never denied me. In my worst moments, in my deepest sin, you have always been near me. You have declared that whoever does not deny you in this world, you will not deny before the Father who is in heaven. Do not allow me to deny you. Do not allow me to deny you in these other people—so much like me in some ways, so much like you in others—whom you have placed along my path. Help me to acknowledge them and serve them. Help me, Lord, because without you I can do nothing. Amen.*

For Group Study

If you are the group leader, plan the session as follows:

Begin by reminding the group of the conversation between Jesus and Peter about what would happen after his betrayal (verses 31-35).

After reading the passage in the Bible, ask the group to compare the three denials, looking at who accused Peter and how he responded in each case. (The purpose is to stress the growing intensity in Peter's denial from one event to the next.)

Say something about how the Judeans regarded Galileans. Explain that, for Judeans, Galileans were not quite as Jewish as they and that they claimed that the Galilean accent was incorrect.

After explaining this, ask the group if they see any hints of this in today's passage.

Turn now to a discussion of the manner in which we divide our own society between "Judeans" and "Galileans." Try to determine in what ways we are "Judeans" and in what ways we are "Galileans."

Explain and discuss with the group what was said earlier: that denying those who are like us, but who are less respected in society, is not only a denial of them but also of ourselves and of Jesus.

End the session by reading and discussing the suggested prayer. After such a discussion, pray those, or other, words with the group.

WEEK
THIRTEEN

3-20-05

First Day: Read Matthew 27:1-14

See: As has already been said, the council of Jewish leaders did not have the authority to decree a death penalty. That is why they scheme together against Jesus in order to bring about his death. To accomplish that, they had to take him before the Roman governor, Pilate, and convince him that Jesus was guilty of some crime that Roman law would punish with death.

Before going on with the story of the trial, Matthew tells us about the remorse of Judas and his attempt to return the money he had received. Verse 6 is interesting, for it shows the strange scruples of the priests. They were the ones who had paid this money in order to have Judas betray Jesus. But now, when they receive it back, they cannot put it in the treasury because it is "blood money."

Beginning with verse 11 we come back to the trial of Jesus. Note that the council has accused Jesus of proclaiming himself "King of the Jews." Since such a claim would be a rebellion against Rome, Jesus is being accused of being a revolutionary.

Judge: Consider the scruples of the priests over what to do with the money Judas has returned to them. They had no scruples about using that money to pay Judas so that he would betray Jesus, his master, and they were not worried about turning Jesus over to the Roman governor. But now they hesitate to place that money in the Temple treasury and have to find another use for it.

Sometimes we have similar scruples. For instance, there are those who will not drink alcohol because they are Christians, but do not give a second thought to the evil that their words and actions do to others. There are those who would not miss church for anything in the world, but then at the service will not sit with "certain people." Others are strict tithers, but then they use the rest of their money irresponsibly and even in activities that destroy their character. In such cases, could we be straining the gnat and swallowing the camel, as Jesus said that the scribes and Pharisees were doing?

Act: As a believer and a student of Scripture, you must have your rules of conduct. Such rules are good and necessary. However, try to discover today which aspects of your life are not covered by such rules. Write down your reflections.

Second Day: Read Matthew 27:15-31 3 -20-05

See: The trial of Jesus lays bare the injustice of society. They accuse him of claiming to be "King of the Jews," although what is understood by that title is very different from what Jesus understands. But each of the participants in the trial is looking after his own interests and not after justice and truth. The chief priests and the elders, after the discussion in the council, have decided to find a way to have the Roman authorities condemn Jesus. They use their powers of persuasion in order to convince the multitude to ask that Barabbas be released and Jesus crucified. Pilate is not very interested in justice. His main concern is the good opinion of his bosses in Rome, and to that effect he wishes to avoid a riot in Jerusalem. That is why he washes his hands, while at the same time pronouncing a verdict that is clearly unjust. (See verse 24, where Pilate says that Jesus is indeed just, but does not defend him, preferring to turn him over to be crucified.)

Judge: What happened to Jesus has also happened to many Christians throughout history. Such was the story of the martyrs of the first centuries. Because they refused to worship the emperor, they were accused of subversion and killed. But this is not just a matter of the past. Even today an unjust world judges all according to its own injustice. The unjust order of the world condemns and even "crucifies" those who do not live according to that order.

We have all known cases in which this has happened, and if we stop to think about it, perhaps we can mention cases in which it has even happened to us.

Let us take an example from daily life. There is a dispute among our fellow workers. We think that both sides are partly wrong and partly right.

But each of the two sides is convinced not only that the other is wrong but also that it is guided by unworthy motives. If we decide, as Christians, that we must try to help each side see the other's position, it is quite possible that both will consider us their enemies, and we will end up in a difficult situation. However, as Christians, that may well be what we have to do.

What happens in the workplace often happens in church also. There are groups prejudiced against each other. It is easy to become a member of one of them, particularly since they are trying to convince us that they are right and the others are wrong. But perhaps what we are to do is to seek a solution, even though this may cause us some difficulties.

Another sphere in which one sees such "unjust judgments" is in Christian social action. We are all agreed that, as Christians, we must do something for the needy. The problem is that we disagree on the best way to fulfill that responsibility. Therefore, so as not to get involved in difficulties with others, very often Christians try to stay away from such issues. But Jesus did not stay away from the problems and struggles of his contemporaries, nor does he stay away from our problems and struggles.

It is precisely this Jesus who did not stay away, and was therefore crucified, who invites us to take the cross and follow him. The cross is a symbol of all the sufferings that Jesus underwent for us. Our cross can be nothing else than the suffering to which Jesus calls us on behalf of others.

We may not like to hear this, but that is what Jesus requires of us.

Act: What are some of the circumstances today, in our church or in our community, where Jesus is calling us to confront injustices similar to those he had to face?

Write down your answers. Pray, committing yourself to confronting some of these situations and asking for strength and direction in doing so.

Third Day: Read Matthew 27:32-37

See: We finally come to the sublime and tragic moment of the Crucifixion. Read the text, looking at each character in the scene.

First mentioned is Simon of Cyrene. Very little is known about him. Mark 15:21 says that he was the father of Alexander and Rufus. That he is mentioned by name, and that Mark gives his sons' names, leads us to suppose that the early readers of the Gospel knew who this man was. Some have suggested that the "Simeon who was called Niger" in Acts 13:1 is this Simon of Cyrene who carried the cross of Jesus.

Think about the others whose names are not given who are the subject of the various sentences in the passage: "They compelled this man to carry his cross"; "they offered him wine to drink"; "they had crucified him"; "they divided his clothes among themselves"; "they sat down there and kept watch over him"; "they put the charge against him." These unnamed people, apparently most of them Roman soldiers, seem to commit cruelty because such is their job, and mocking Jesus, they put a sign over his head proclaiming him to be "King of the Jews."

Judge: There are many ways of coming to Jesus. Some look from afar and never approach. This is what happens with most people who hear the gospel and think that it is a good thing but never make a commitment. Others come from afar and approach slowly. Others are so involved in the sinful order around them and in the injustice of the world that they are like those soldiers who crucified Jesus because they were ordered to do so, or like those who mocked him.

Then there is Simon of Cyrene, who was forced to carry the cross, and apparently eventually became a disciple and perhaps even a leader among Christians.

Today there are similar cases. For instance, I know a woman who knew of some illiterate people in her neighborhood and felt compelled to teach them to read (just as Simon found himself compelled to carry the cross). After a short time, she became increasingly involved with them and with the church that provided her with material and room for her classes. Eventually, this woman who had walked by that church with no interest for many years became president of its women's society.

How did you come to the cross?

Have you actually approached, or are you still looking from afar?

If you are looking from afar, come closer; and perhaps like Simon of Cyrene you will suddenly find yourself carrying the cross and finding life in it.

Act: Make a list of the things in your life that keep you from taking up the cross. Pray about each of them, asking that God will give you power and freedom to approach the cross. As you feel that your prayer is answered about each of them, cross it out.

3-20-05

Fourth Day: Read Matthew 27:38-56

See: Continue contemplating this scene, and see those who stand around the cross. Now almost everybody mocks. Those who pass, ridicule him, shaking their heads. The religious leaders who planned his death, "the chief priests also, along with the scribes and elders, were mocking him." Even those who are being crucified next to him deride him.

However, even behind the mockery of those who do not understand (and of those who do not wish to understand), the drama of all ages is unfolding. Not only the entire Gospel of Matthew but also the entire biblical tradition leads to this point. It was for this that God called Abraham out of the land of his ancestors. It was for this that the angel struggled with Jacob. It was for this that Israel was brought out of Egypt. It was for this that the prophets spoke. It was for this, the Crucifixion.

Beginning with verse 51, Matthew describes events that are intended to be a glimpse of the significance of what is taking place here.

Eventually, the leader of the soldiers who were crucifying him declares with reluctant terror, "Truly this man was God's Son" (verse 54).

While all of this is taking place, the women who had followed Jesus from Galilee and had provided for him (see the beginning of Luke 8) stand there, although from afar.

Judge: At this point, a common question is Why did Jesus die? In times past, some Christians have answered that the Jews killed him. That is untrue on several counts. First of all, those who actually killed him were Romans, not Jews. Second, although those who conspired to have him arrested and killed were indeed Jews, so were Jesus and all of his disciples. Even more so, if it is in any sense true that Jesus died for our redemption, then we must also say that it is each one of us that is the cause for his death.

Some look from a distance, like the women. Others, like the disciples, have even fled and hid. Others, precisely because they will not accept the challenge of the cross, mock the Crucified. Some of us, by the grace of God, have believed. But for each and every one of us, for those who are far as well as for those who were near, Jesus died on the cross.

Act: Just as earlier we practiced a prayer of "absolute silence," try now to act in "absolute calm," letting God be the one who acts in you. Decide nothing. Simply remember Jesus Christ, crucified for you. Stand by those who pass and chuckle. Stand by the thieves who mock. Stand by the religious chiefs who rejoice in their victory. Look at Jesus Christ, crucified for you. Give thanks and ask for forgiveness. Let him be the one who speaks. Continue in silence, without a word even to yourself.

In your mind, approach Jesus on the cross. Get so close to him that you can see the world as it would have appeared from atop the cross. Look at your life. Look at what you did yesterday, what you plan to do tomorrow. Look at your life from the cross, and stand in awesome wonder at God's forgiving mercy.

End with a prayer of thanksgiving.

Fifth Day: Read Matthew 27:57-66 3 -20 -05

See: The passage divides naturally into two parts: The first part (verses 57-61) tells us about the steps taken by those close to Jesus (Joseph of Arimathea, Mary Magdalene, and the other Mary) to bury his body and to accompany him to the grave. The second part (verses 62-66) tells how "the chief priests and the Pharisees" went before Pilate telling him of the danger that the word might circulate that Jesus had risen from the dead.

Once again, the argument is political: If such a word circulates, there will certainly be the type of riots and disorders which Pilate fears, and which may bring criticism from his bosses in Rome. The result is that, under the direction of the Judean religious leadership, a Roman guard is placed before the tomb.

Judge: Think about these people, religious leaders of the nation, who take steps to make sure that Jesus does not rise from the dead. Their interests and commitments are such that they cannot even allow for a rumor of resurrection. They have to guard against it, and they do this by sealing the site and guarding the tomb with Roman soldiers. For centuries God has been preparing the people for this hour, and now the leaders of the people cannot accept it.

But do not just think about those who could not accept the joy of the Resurrection because their interests and commitments did not allow them to do so. Today there are many in the same situation. They are so committed to sin that they cannot even imagine the possibility that sin may be destroyed. Some even live by sin, profiting from it, and fear that the new life in Christ will be the end of their sustenance. Therefore they prefer, first, to mock (as we saw yesterday), and then, to refuse to believe (as we see today).

Act: Remember that you are a follower of the one who, seeing the crowds, had compassion for them. Have compassion for those who do not believe. Commit yourself to approaching them. Do this with words of joy and hope, not of bitterness or condemnation. Let them discover the enormity of their own sin when they face the crucified Lord. Your task is to show them the immensity of God's love.

Sixth Day: Read Matthew 28:1-15

See: We come to the climax of our study and of the entire Gospel narrative—Easter. Very often we think that the center of the Gospel is the Crucifixion and that Easter is the mere confirmation that Jesus is, in truth, God's Son. In that case, Easter becomes a sort of "stamp of approval" from God. But Easter is much more than that. It is part of the saving work of Jesus. It is the beginning of victory. It is the inauguration of God's reign.

In light of all this, it is surprising to see that Easter causes fear, not only among the enemies of Jesus (as we saw today with the guards who appear to be dead) but also in the case of the followers of Jesus.

The text speaks repeatedly of the fear of the women who were the first disciples to hear the message of Easter. The angel tells them not to fear. Even so, they leave the tomb with a combination of "fear and great joy." When they eventually meet Jesus, after they embrace his feet and worship him, he once again tells them, "Do not be afraid."

Judge: If we really understand the scope of the message of Easter, it certainly is overwhelming. Without that message, the years that the disciples have spent following Jesus are nothing but a sad mistake. All that they have to do now is return to their homes and their nets, tell their friends and neighbors that they made a mistake, and begin rebuilding their lives. That is difficult. But more difficult still is what will happen if Jesus is raised from the dead. If Easter is true, then all that he said about taking the cross and following him, about losing their lives, about the hard road and the narrow gate, all of that is also true.

Think about that in concrete terms. Elizabeth is a Christian. In her work there are others who are not Christians. Because the Lord has risen, she knows that she is to give witness in her workplace. It would be much simpler not to give such a witness; but the Risen One demands it. Perhaps her witness creates problems for her at work. She does not seek such problems, and she correctly tries to make her witness as joyful and as accepting as possible. Still, there are problems. She is already on the path to the cross, but she can do this joyfully because behind the cross stands the Lord who rose again from the dead.

Kevin is also a Christian. His boss is treating a fellow worker unjustly. It would be normal, and also easy, to remain silent and not take the risk. But the Lord is risen. A new world of peace, love, and justice has been proclaimed. Therefore, Kevin must protest, even if he risks his own employment. This causes him fear and concern. But beyond the concerns and difficulties, he has been called by the Lord who triumphed over the cross. The fear of losing his job is overcome by the joy of Easter.

Act: Consider: How would your life be different if Christ had not risen from the dead? If there is no difference, perhaps you have not taken Easter seriously enough. Write in your notebook the following words, and complete the sentence: *Because the Lord is risen, I . . .* Repeat it several times, each time writing down a different result of the resurrection of Jesus.

Seventh Day: Read Matthew 28:16-20   5-22-05

See: This passage is known as "The Commissioning of the Disciples," or "The Great Commission," and has been one of the springboards of Christian missionary work throughout the ages. A very important word that we often ignore is the "therefore" in verse 19. What follows that word is a consequence of what precedes them. Jesus tells them that "all authority" has been given to him, and in order to underline the full scope of that authority he tells them that this is "in heaven and on earth." There is nothing beyond the reach of his authority, and that is the reason the disciples are to go and make more disciples. They are not going out to increase the authority of Jesus as he gains more followers. Jesus is already Lord, no matter how many people believe in him.

Note also the relationship between this passage and the one we studied yesterday. There the Lord, through the women, told the disciples to go back to Galilee, where he now gives them this "Commission." The disciples are to begin where Jesus began: at home in Galilee. This is a sign that their lives will be similar to that of Jesus—lives of service leading them to crosses, but also to Easter.

Finally, the phrase "to the end of the age" can also mean the end of the world, the last corner of the earth, the most distant and desolate place we might imagine. Thus, "the end" in which Jesus still promises his company is both geographic and temporal, for it also refers to the final moment when all promises will be fulfilled. Therefore, over both time and space, the Lord to whom belongs "all authority" promises his company to those who go in his name.

Judge: This means that we are mistaken if we think that when we preach the gospel we are somehow expanding the authority of Jesus. What we do, and that only thanks to the action of the Holy Spirit, is to increase the number of disciples who acknowledge and accept his authority. But Jesus is Lord, and that does not depend on any human being, nor does it become more or less true depending on how many people believe it.

When we go out to make disciples, we do so because Jesus Christ is already Lord. We go out to proclaim and to help people realize and accept the fact that all authority, in heaven as well as on earth, is his.

But, if that is the case, it means that our lives must also be guided by that principle. If the authority is already in the hands of Jesus, we can seek the reign of God and its justice. We can take the cross and follow him. We can go wherever God sends us, for Jesus is already there, waiting for us long before we arrive.

But there is more. If Jesus is Lord of all that exists, this means that whenever we go some place in order to witness for him, he is already Lord of that place. Therefore, our task is not only to speak about him but also to discover his presence already there.

Consider a case. Ann is a missionary and is devoted to evangelizing, that is, to "making disciples." One day she enters a very poor house where there is misery and where the husband physically abuses his wife. Certainly, such a home needs Jesus Christ. But even there Ann sees that this woman, with no system of support such as the church and in the midst of all her poverty and suffering, loves her little daughter. She protects and nourishes her. She does not allow her husband to hurt her. The poor woman, in spite of being beaten, is ready to give her life for that daughter. In spite of the misery in that house, and of all the evil that exists in it, Ann as a Christian must see in the love of that woman for her daughter a reflection of the love of Jesus Christ, and she will know that in some mysterious way, even in the midst of such tragic circumstances, Jesus is looking for a way to employ his authority for the good of this family. On that basis, Ann can now relate to the woman as a sister, not only in love but also in respect. Therefore, every time Ann enters such a household and finds Jesus waiting there for her, it is an opportunity for growth in faith, not only for those who live in that house but also for Ann herself.

Act: Think about a place where you have not dared give witness for fear that it would not be accepted. Be certain that even this place is under Jesus' authority. With that knowledge, decide to go there as soon as possible and witness for Jesus Christ, who is not only Lord of your life and of the church but also of that place, even though those who are there may rebel against him.

If there are others who have been following this study about Matthew, gather with them so that you may discuss how to give such witness jointly.

Since this is the last of your studies with Matthew, review what you have written in your notebook; and on the last page of your reflections on Matthew, write down the most important thing you have learned. Decide to share it with other people both in your church and outside.

For Group Study

Make use of this opportunity to review with the group what has been discussed and learned during these *Three Months with Matthew*. To that end you may suggest that, since you are being sent to make disciples, it would be good for us to create a sort of "curriculum for discipleship." This would be a list of things that, according to the Gospel of Matthew, seem to be fundamental for discipleship.

Ask the group to make a list of the things they have learned from Matthew as being important for discipleship. As the group mentions each point, write it down on a large sheet of paper so that all can read it.

Since this will be your last session, proclaim it to be a "graduation ceremony," and discuss a possible way to celebrate the completion of these three months.